Activities *for* English Language Learners Across *the* Curriculum

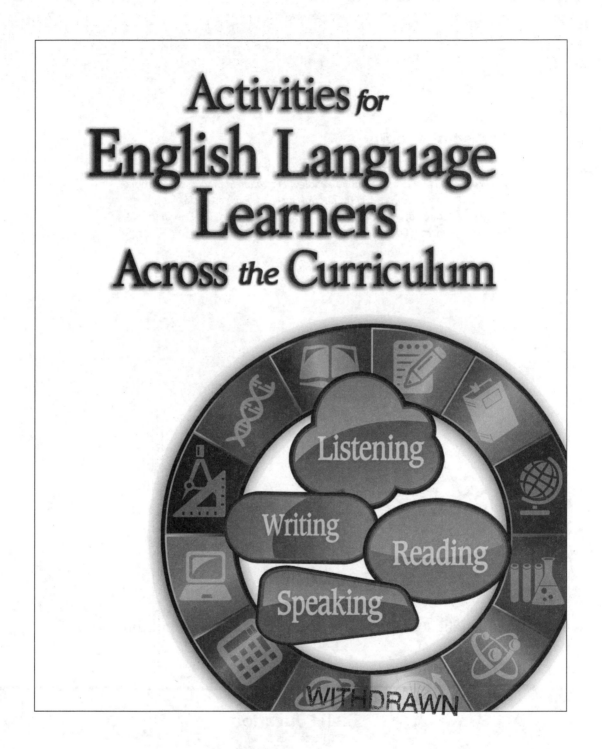

Author

Stephen A. White, Ph.D.

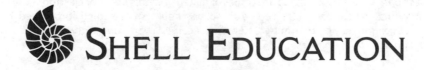

SHELL EDUCATION

Publishing Credits

Dona Herweck Rice, *Editor-in-Chief*; Lee Aucoin, *Creative Director*; Don Tran, *Print Production Manager*; Timothy J. Bradley, *Illustration Manager*; Lori Kamola, M.S.Ed and Conni Medina, M.S.Ed, *Editorial Directors*; Evelyn Garcia, *Associate Editor*; Lee Aucoin, *Cover Designer*; Robin Erickson, *Interior Layout Designer*; Corinne Burton, M.S. Ed., *Publisher*

Copyright 2004 McRel. www.mcrel.org/standards-benchmarks.

Shell Education
5301 Oceanus Drive
Huntington Beach, CA 92649-1030
http://www.shelleducation.com
ISBN 978-1-4258-0203-5
©2010 Shell Educational Publishing, Inc.

Table of Contents

Introduction

Preface 5
Research 6
Proficiency Levels for English Language Learners 8
Bloom's Taxonomy and Differentiation 10
How to Use This Book 16
Differentiating Lessons by Proficiency Level 19
Example Lesson by Proficiency Level 20
Standards Correlations 25
Correlation to TESOL Standards 26
Correlation to McREL Standards 27

Reading

Activities Log 32
ABCs 33
A Live Book Report 35
Circle Spelling 36
Fill in the Squares 37
Bright Idea 39
Dissect a Newspaper 41
Performing Fairy Tales 42
Sequenced Bookmarks 43
Study an Author 44
Three in a Row 46
Tricky Word Flags 48
What's the Title? 50

Writing

Activities Log 51
ABCs 52
Acting Out Antonyms 54
Action-Play Compound Word Story 55
Name It! 56
Brainstorming Blanks 58
Category Race 59
Change the Words 60
Holiday Story Starters 62
The Longest Sentence 63
Object Stories 64
So-Close Pictures 65
The Fewest Clues 67
Idiom Pictures 69
Word Changes 71
World's Longest Story 73

Mathematics

Activities Log 74
ABCs 75
Countdown 77
Three in a Row 78
Daily Math Question 80
Math Words 81
Let Your Fingers Do the Walking on the Calendar 83
Math Circle Memory 85
Math High Five 86
Math Stand-Up 88
Math King/Queen 89
Scavenger Hunt. 91
Time Directions. 92

Science

Activities Log 94
ABCs 95
Auditory Memory Game. 97
Bingo 98
Science Maze. 100
Science Similes 102
Science Swap. 103
Science Synonyms 104
Science Vocabulary 106
Secret Science Box. 108
Textures 109
Three in a Row 110
True/False Science 112

Social Studies

Activities Log 114
ABCs 115
Famous People Similes 117
Clothing Comparison 118
Scavenger Hunt. 119
School Directions. 120
Secret Words 122
State Riddles 123
Telephone Role-Play 124
Three in a Row 126
Which Ocean, Which Continent? 128

References Cited. 130
Teacher Resource CD. 131

Preface

I have been in the field of education for 35 years as a classroom teacher, director, and state and national consultant. I began my teaching career in the Boston Public Schools. My first day on the job, an ESL student showed up on the doorstep of our middle school. The administration wasn't sure what to do, except to place the student in my Spanish class and hope for the best. After a month of school, I had 34 students who didn't speak English. All of these students spoke Spanish. I am not sure what the school would have done if they had spoken any other language. As time went on, other students from different languages were added to the ESL program.

I gave up my conference period to teach ESL because I had a full load of Spanish classes before the year began. My ESL students got placed into all content-area subjects. Regular content-area teachers would come down the hall to my classroom, asking me to translate their materials into Spanish. They would also ask, "When you have a moment, could you call Maria's parents to tell them she wasn't doing her work?" or other similar requests. I am sure this sounds familiar to many ESL teachers.

In 1973, there weren't a lot of materials or activities that were appropriate for my ESL class. Therefore I had to invent the wheel. I had to come up with activities not only for my ESL class, but also for the other content areas. At the time, it was a lot of work, but I realized that by providing activities at my students' proficiency and functional levels in the content areas, they learned English much faster.

For the past 15 years I have been traveling across the United States and internationally as well, presenting at school districts and local, state, national, and international conferences. Each time I presented, I had several teachers ask me, "Dr. White, do you have these activities in a book?" Unfortunately, I would have to reply, "No." Finally, I can say that I have had the time to put these activities into one comprehensive book.

This book has been designed to provide educators with diverse classroom activities that will help meet English language learners' educational needs. It includes a variety of strategies that support opportunities for the following: building academic vocabulary, increasing comprehension, developing oral language, developing socialization, cooperative learning, building and activating prior knowledge, and informal assessment with progress monitoring.

All of the activities in this book are based on students' language proficiency needs and have been successfully used in my classroom. The key to success with these activities is to know the proficiency level of your students and the appropriate questions to ask students at that proficiency level. I wish you all the best as you try these activities with your students.

Stephen A. White, Ph.D.

Research

The number of English language learners has grown dramatically over the past 30 years, and the numbers continue to increase. In the United States alone, English language learners comprise 10.5 percent of the nation's K–12 enrollment (National Institute of Child Health and Human Development 2006). There are many English language learners around the world, too. According to the British Council, by 2010 there could be approximately 2 billion people learning English (Graddol 2006). By definition, **an English language learner is someone who is acquiring English and has a first language other than English** (National Council of Teachers of English 2008). Depending on where you teach, these students might be referred to as Limited English Proficient (LEP), English as a Second Language (ESL), English Learner (EL), Culturally and Linguistically Diverse (CLD), English as a Foreign Language (EFL), or Dual Language Learner (DLL). In this book, these students will be referred to as English language learners (ELL).

For many teachers, our classrooms look very different today from how they looked 10 years ago. They are filled with students from a variety of linguistic and culturally diverse backgrounds. We have the challenge of figuring out how to teach them effectively and providing an environment where all students can succeed.

Oral language proficiency is the first step in the language learning process. Oral language is defined as speaking and listening skills. English language learners are able to attain word-level skills (decoding, word recognition, and spelling) regardless of their oral-language proficiency. However, an English language learner's ability to comprehend text and to develop writing skills is dependent on his or her oral-language proficiency. Therefore, "vocabulary knowledge, listening comprehension, syntactic skills and the ability to handle meta-linguistic aspects of language, such as being able to provide the definitions of words, are linked to English reading and writing proficiency" (August and Shanahan 2006). First-language oral proficiency has a positive impact on developmental patterns in second-language speech discrimination and production, intra-word segmentation, and vocabulary. **This book provides teachers with a wide variety of activities needed to help students develop proficiency in English.**

Students move through stages of **language acquisition** as they develop their language proficiency. Different states call these levels of proficiency by different names, and some states may vary with their number of levels. However, all students move through the same stages of language acquisition as they become proficient in English. **Teachers should be aware of the distinctive characteristics that each stage has in order to effectively differentiate to meet students' needs.**

Research *(cont.)*

These stages are clearly outlined in the book *The Natural Approach* by Krashen and Terrell. The first stage is the **Preproduction** stage, and it is known as the "silent period" because ELLs will most likely remain silent during this stage. This stage has an approximate time frame of zero to six months. The next stage, **Early Production**, has an approximate time frame between six months to one year. Students at this stage have very limited comprehension and will most likely produce one or two word answers. **Speech Emergence** is the third stage, and the approximate time frame is one to three years. Students at this stage are developing good comprehension, however frequently make grammar and pronunciation errors. At the fourth stage, **Intermediate Fluency**, the approximate time frame is three to five years. Students are now capable of stating sentences of increasing length and complexity. The final stage is **Advanced Fluency**. Students at this stage have a near-native level of speech. This stage has an approximate time frame of five to seven years (Krashen and Terrell 1983).

Students will pass through the five stages, however the length that it takes students to pass through each stage will vary. It is known that on average, academic language can take at least five to seven years to develop, and it can take even longer for a student who was not literate in their primary language when starting school (Collier and Thomas 1989). **The activities in this book have been created with these stages in mind and support students at all levels of language proficiency.**

The activities in this book were designed using SDAIE (Specially Designed Academic Instruction in English), an approach to help English language learners access content-area curriculum. With SDAIE strategies, students have the opportunity to learn the subject matter and meet grade-level standards while also increasing proficiency in English (Jimenez 2009). SDAIE instruction uses many effective techniques, which you will find throughout the activities in this book. Throughout the reading, writing, mathematics, science, and social studies sections, you will find activities to support the use of **background building**, **vocabulary development**, **visuals**, **realia** (real objects), **graphic organizers**, and **manipulatives** (hands-on materials). Students have many opportunities to **build their oral and written language skills** through repetition and review, and by working in groups and with partners to practice speaking in various settings (Jimenez 2009).

Proficiency Levels for English Language Learners

All teachers should know the levels of language proficiency for each of their English language learners. Knowing these levels will help to plan instruction. (The category titles and numbers of levels vary from district to district or state to state, but the general descriptions are common.) Students at level 1 will need a lot of language support in all the activities, especially during instruction. Using visuals to support oral and written language will help make the language more comprehensible. These students "often understand much more than they are able to express" (Herrell and Jordan 2004). It is the teacher's job to move them from just listening to language to expressing language. Students at levels 2 and 3 will benefit from pair work in speaking tasks, but they will need additional individual support during writing and reading tasks. Students at levels 4 and 5 (or 6, in some cases) may appear to be fully proficient in the English language. However, because they are English language learners, they may still struggle with comprehending the academic language used during instruction. They may also struggle with reading and writing.

The following chart shows the proficiency levels for English language learners at a quick glance. These proficiency levels are based on the World-Class Instructional Design and Assessment (WIDA) Consortium (WIDA 2007).

Proficiency Levels at a Quick Glance

Proficiency Level	Questions to Ask	Activities/Actions		
Level 1— Beginning (Entering) minimal comprehension no verbal production	Where is…? What is the main idea? What examples do you see? What are the parts of…? Which was your favorite…? What would be different if…?	listen	draw	mime
		point	circle	respond (with one or two words)
Level 2— Early Intermediate (Beginning) limited comprehension short spoken phrases	Can you list three…? Tell me. What facts or ideas show…? When will you use…? How is…related to…? What is your opinion of…? What way would you design…?	move	select	act/act out
		match	choose	list

Proficiency Levels for English Language Learners (cont.)

Proficiency Level	Questions to Ask	Activities/Actions		
Level 3—Intermediate (Developing) increased comprehension simple sentences	How did…happen? Which is the best answer…? What do you already know about…? Why do you think…? How would you evaluate…? What would happen if…?	name	list	respond (with phrases or sentences)
		label	categorize	paraphrase
		tell/say	analyze	justify
Level 4—Early Advanced (Expanding) very good comprehension some errors in speech	How would you show…? How would you summarize…? What would result if…? What is the relationship between…? Would it be better if…? What is an alternative…?	recall	retell	define
		compare/contrast	explain	restate
		describe	role-play	create
Level 5—Advanced (Bridging) comprehension comparable to native-English speakers speaks using complex sentences	What were the most obvious…? What is true about…? How would you use…? What ideas justify…? How would you have advised…? How would you improve…?	analyze	defend	complete
		evaluation	justify	support
		create	describe	express

Bloom's Taxonomy and Differentiation

Bloom's Taxonomy has been used in classrooms for more than 40 years as a hierarchy of questions that progress from less to more complex. The progression allows teachers to identify the levels at which students are thinking. It also provides a framework for introducing a variety of questions to all students. In schools today, most emphasis is placed on ensuring lessons, curriculum, and materials cover all of these levels. A 1992 report found that in the language programs studied, teachers had a tendency to ask low-level questions during instructional time (Ramirez 1992). While students at the first level of language acquisition will benefit from these questions because of their lower level, these students also need to be challenged to think more deeply. Knowing the various levels of language acquisition and asking appropriate questions for students at each level will engage them and increase oral language development.

The original Bloom's Taxonomy identifies three domains of knowledge: **cognitive**, **affective**, and **psychomotor**. The taxonomy begins at the lowest level and then progresses towards evaluation. The lowest three levels are: **knowledge**, **comprehension**, and **application**. The highest three levels are: **analysis**, **synthesis**, and **evaluation**. In 2002, a new updated Bloom's Taxonomy was created to reflect 21st century skills. The words of the taxonomy were changed from nouns (such as knowledge) to verbs (such as remembering), and the order of the two highest levels of thinking were switched.

Here is a comparison of the original Bloom's Taxonomy to the new Bloom's Taxonomy:

Original Bloom's Taxonomy	New Bloom's Taxonomy
Knowledge	Remembering
Comprehension	Understanding
Application	Applying
Analysis	Analyzing
Synthesis	Evaluating
Evaluation	Creating

Additionally, with the new Bloom's Taxonomy, instead of just identifying the three domains of cognitive, affective, and psychomotor knowledge, there are two main dimensions: the **knowledge dimension** (knowledge) and the **cognitive process dimension** (how knowledge is demonstrated). The new Bloom's Taxonomy breaks the knowledge domain into four types: **factual**, **conceptual**, **procedural**, and **meta-cognitive** (Anderson and Krathwohl 2001).

This book utilizes the new Bloom's Taxonomy, which aligns with 21st century skills. If you are teaching with the original Bloom's Taxonomy, refer to the chart above to correlate to your curriculum.

Questions are provided on the following pages, listed by level of language proficiency. To **differentiate instruction**, first think about the student or group of students you are trying to target, and **determine their level(s) of language proficiency**. Then, within that level, **choose questions** at the various levels of Bloom's Taxonomy to challenge students to think more deeply. This method can be used with all of your students, varying the questions based on your students' levels of language proficiency.

Bloom's Taxonomy and Differentiation *(cont.)*
New Bloom's Taxonomy Questions by Levels of Proficiency

Beginning Level (Entering)	
Remembering	
Why did...?	Where is...?
Which one...?	How is...?
What is...?	What happened...?
Who is...?	Can you find...? Show me.
Understanding	
What is the main idea...?	How is...different from...?
Which statement supports...?	In your own words, what is...?
What is the pattern in...?	What are the steps...?
What were the reasons...?	What does it remind you of...?
Applying	
What examples do you see...?	How would you use...?
What other way could you...?	What could you change about...?
What do...have in common?	How could you find out more about...?
What questions do you have about...?	What else does...make you think about?
Analyzing	
What are the parts of...?	What group does...belong to?
What is your guess about...?	How are...and...the same?
What is the rule about...?	Why is...?
How could...be simpler?	What is out of place with...?
Evaluating	
Do you agree with the actions...? Why or why not?	What do you think of the way...ended?
Which was your favorite...?	What was good/bad about...?
How could you test...?	What is another way you could...?
How could you put together...?	Have you changed your mind about...? Why or why not?
Creating	
What would be different if...?	What changes would you make...?
What would be a better choice...?	What way would you design...?
What is most important about...?	Can you imagine a new...? Why or why not?
What would someone else think about...?	Is there a different way to solve...? Tell me.

Bloom's Taxonomy and Differentiation *(cont.)*
New Bloom's Taxonomy Questions by Levels of Proficiency *(cont.)*

Early Intermediate Level (Beginning)	
Remembering	
Can you choose...? Show me.	Can you list the three...? Tell me.
How would you tell about...which one...?	What are the qualities of...?
What did you notice about...?	What do you recall about...?
Can you find examples of...? Show me.	What details did you notice about...?
Understanding	
What facts or ideas show...?	What can you say about...?
What is the main idea of...?	How would you compare...?
What is similar to/different from...?	How would you summarize...?
What were the causes of...?	What comes next in the sequence/pattern...?
Applying	
What examples can you find to...?	How would you organize...to solve...?
How can you make use of the facts...?	When will you use...?
What would you need to...?	What is the relationship between...and...?
What connection can you make between...?	Could this have happened in...? Why or why not?
Analyzing	
How is...related to...?	Why do you think...?
What is the theme...?	What are the parts...?
How would you classify...?	Can you identify the different parts...? What are they?
How would you break down...?	What is a synonym/antonym for...?
Evaluating	
What is your opinion of...?	Would it be better if...? Why or why not?
What would you recommend...?	How would you rate the...?
What would be the impact of...?	What are the advantages/disadvantages of...?
Can you rank the...? Show me.	Which outcome is better for...?
Creating	
Can you invent...? Why or why not?	How would you adapt...to create a different...?
What way would you design...?	Suppose you could...what would you do...?
How could you show it as a picture/movement/song...?	How could you combine...?
What would have happened if...?	What else could you use for...?

Bloom's Taxonomy and Differentiation (cont.)

New Bloom's Taxonomy Questions by Levels of Proficiency (cont.)

Intermediate Level (Developing)	
Remembering	
How did...happen?	Why did...?
Where did...?	Who were the main...?
When did...happen?	Who was...?
Which one was...?	What did you notice about...?
Understanding	
How would you rephrase...?	Which statement supports...?
Which is the best answer...?	How would you summarize...?
How would you compare...with...?	How do you outline...?
If you were a reporter, how would you explain...?	What is your definition of...?
Applying	
How would you use...?	What examples can you find to...?
How would you organize...to show...?	How would you apply what you learned to develop...?
What would you ask in an interview with...?	What could you do to improve the...?
What do you already know about...?	What principle could you apply...?
Analyzing	
How would you classify the type of...?	Why do you think...?
What motive is there...?	What conclusions can you draw...?
What evidence can you find...?	What inference can you make...?
Which characteristics show...?	What else would you categorize as...?
Evaluating	
Do you agree with the author...? With the outcome...?	How would you prove...? Disprove...?
How would you evaluate...?	What choice would you have made...?
How would you rate the...?	If you could change..., would you...?
Was...better or worse because of...?	Which was the most valuable lesson...?
Creating	
What changes would you make to solve...?	What would happen if...?
What could be done to minimize/maximize...?	If you could..., what would you do...?
What facts can you add to change...?	How would...have impacted...?
What conclusion would someone else draw from...?	How would someone else solve...?

Bloom's Taxonomy and Differentiation *(cont.)*
New Bloom's Taxonomy Questions by Levels of Proficiency *(cont.)*

Early Advanced Level (Expanding)	
Remembering	
Who were the main…?	When did…happen?
How would you explain…?	How would you show…?
What do you recall…?	What would you list…?
How would you describe…?	Which is true about…?
Understanding	
What type is…?	How would you compare…? Contrast…?
How will you state or interpret in your own words…?	How do you explain what is happening…? What is meant…?
How would you summarize…?	How do you define…?
What is the order of…?	What are the reasons that…?
Applying	
How would you solve…using what you've learned…?	How would you show your understanding of…?
What approach would you use to…?	What would result if…?
How could you use…for…?	Could this have happened in…? Why or why not?
Can you model how…? Show me.	What is a metaphor for…?
Analyzing	
What distinguishes…from…?	What inference can you make…?
What conclusions can you draw…?	Can you identify the different parts…? What are they?
What is the relationship between…?	What are the qualities of…?
Describe the properties of…?	How would you group…?
Evaluating	
What is the value or importance of…?	Would it be better if…?
Why did he or she (the character) choose…?	What would you cite to defend those actions…?
Based on what you know, how would you explain…?	How would you justify…?
How would you compare the ideas…?	How would…change the outcome…?
Creating	
How would you elaborate on the reason…?	What is an alternative…?
What could be combined to improve/change…?	If you could…, what would you do?
What facts can you compile to disprove…?	What is an original way for the…?
Is there an experiment to test for…?	What would the consequences be if…?

Bloom's Taxonomy and Differentiation *(cont.)*
New Bloom's Taxonomy Questions by Levels of Proficiency *(cont.)*

Advanced Level (Bridging)	
Remembering	
Which events show…?	What are the dates of…?
Which characters…?	What is the order of…?
How would you picture the…?	What were the most obvious…?
Which…was emphasized in…?	What is the pertinent…?
Understanding	
How did…get to…?	Why did…?
What interpretation can you find…?	What facts or ideas prove…?
What is happening…? What is meant…?	What is true about…?
How would you summarize…?	What were the results when…?
Applying	
How would you use…?	How could you demonstrate…?
What factors impact the outcome…?	What is the lesson to be learned about…?
What life lesson is revealed when…?	Which situation exemplifies…?
How could you analogize…?	How does…affect…?
Analyzing	
How is…related to…?	Which arguments support…?
What clues led you to infer…?	What previous experience impacted your view of…?
What are the different parts…?	What ideas justify…?
Are there other ways to defend…?	How many perspectives…?
Evaluating	
How would you have advised…?	Whose judgment is best about…?
How would you assess the importance of…?	How would you defend a different…?
What was sacrificed when…?	What would have been gained by…?
What if…had never…?	Why was it better that…?
Creating	
What is an alternative plan if…?	How would you improve…?
Is there a different expression for…?	How might…alter the outcome…?
How would you change/modify the plan…?	What unusual factors might influence…?
What theory would you formulate for…?	How would you move logically…?

How to Use This Book

Ready to Use Ideas and Activities

The activities in this book will help teachers provide differentiated ideas necessary for students to improve their English while they learn. As you are reading through the activities, remember that all students learn at their own rates, so it is important to build student's self-esteem and self-confidence as they learn English.

The reproducible activity sheets will challenge and entertain your students. Many of the activities in this book integrate language arts with other subject areas. Making connections between the disciplines can help students learn and retain more.

The activities are varied to provide students with different learning settings. Besides whole-group instruction, opportunities for small-group instruction, partner projects, and independent learning are provided.

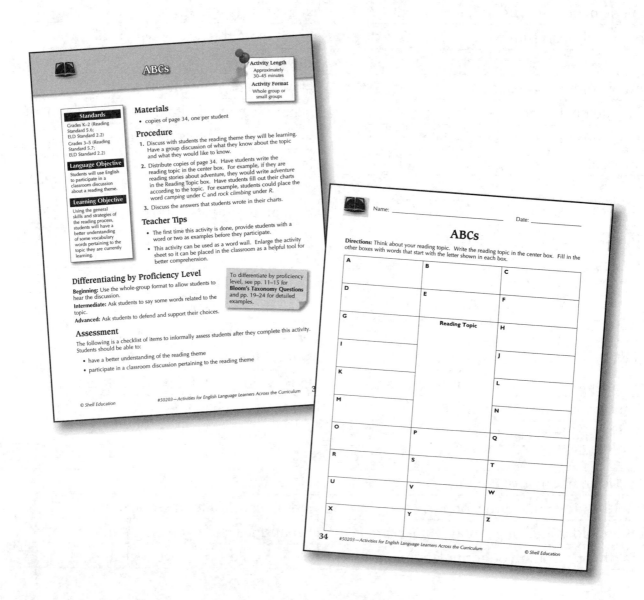

How to Use This Book *(cont.)*

The following provides a more detailed overview of the various components of this book and how to use it most effectively.

Before using the activities in this book, the teacher should know the students' levels of proficiency. Schools or districts often assess English language learners to determine this information. Knowing the students' levels of proficiency, teachers can make the needed modifications (see pages 19–24).

Following this guide, there are five examples of the ABCs activity at different proficiency levels (pages 20–24) that will show you specifically how to incorporate the various levels into the lesson. The examples follow the exact format that is used throughout the book with all of the activities. This guide is a walk-through to show you the various components of an activity, as well as how to properly follow the format for incorporating Bloom's Taxonomy.

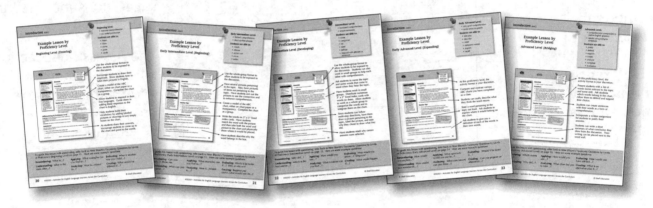

At the beginning of every subject area, there is an **Activities Log** page. This page is for teachers to keep a record of when they taught the activities and what adjustments or modifications were made. It is always a good idea to use this log as a reflection. By doing so, it will allow teachers to keep track of student progress, as well as to write any additional modifications that may need to be made in the future.

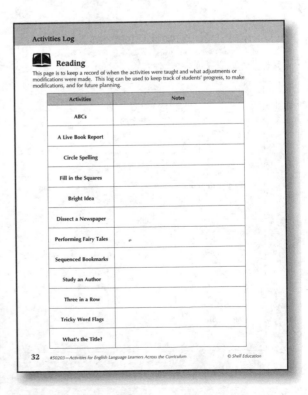

How to Use This Book *(cont.)*

Standards and **Objectives** are listed for each activity. The objectives will let you know specifically the area of focus for a given activity.

Procedures are provided for each activity to let you know exactly how the activity should flow.

It is important to remember to differentiate. See the **Differentiating by Proficiency Level** section and pages 19–24.

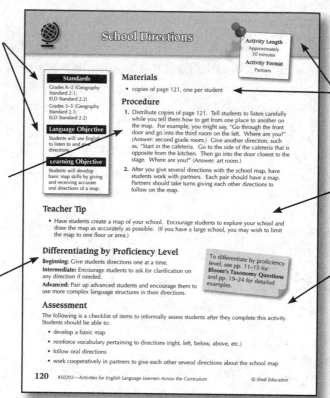

Activity Length, **Activity Format**, and **Materials** are listed in all the activities to help plan out the lesson.

Teacher Tips are classroom-tested suggestions included in every activity.

The **Assessment** section tells what you can informally assess to provide you with a better understanding of student comprehension.

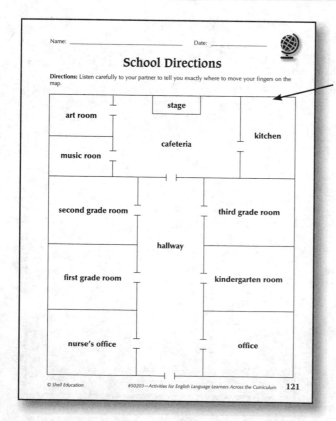

Some lessons have reproducible **activity pages** that follow the lesson page. They are also provided on the Teacher Resource CD.

Differentiating Lessons by Proficiency Level

The following pages will show you one activity titled "ABCs" and how the five levels of proficiency and question stems are integrated into the activity. Use these pages as a guide to differentiate instruction by language proficiency levels to meet the needs of English language learners in your class.

The first example lesson by proficiency level is for the **Beginning Level (Entering)**. The list at the top of the page shows some characteristics common to these students (minimal comprehension and no verbal production). The list also shows the actions that students can do at this proficiency level (listen, draw, mime, point, and circle). The list from this table comes from the proficiency chart on page 8.

Under the list is the activity "ABCs." This activity is found in each content area of the book to show how to integrate multiple subjects. Notice the arrows pointing inward to the activity from the various recommendations. These recommendations are important in understanding how modifications can be made to meet students at the **Beginning Level (Entering)**. For example, the arrow next to step one, under the Procedure section directs the teacher to encourage students to draw their responses and label their pictures in English. Looking back to the list at the top, you will notice that students at this level have no verbal production. Offering the opportunity for students to draw their answers will provide them with the opportunity to communicate their ideas. Labeling their drawings with your guidance is beneficial in building their vocabulary. Take a look at the other recommendations and how they correlate with the information in the list at the top of the page.

At the bottom of the example activity is a list of questions that were selected from the proficiency chart located on page 11. You may also notice that these questions are just a few examples of the various new Bloom's Taxonomy questions. The questions listed were selected for the **Beginning Level (Entering)**. Choose questions at the various levels of Bloom's Taxonomy to challenge students to think deeply. For example, the first level listed is *Remembering*. The example provided is, "What is…?" Looking back to the list at the top, you will notice that students at this level are able to point. If you were to ask the student this question, the possibility of them being able to answer is likely since an action the student may do at this level is point. Take a look at the other questions and how they also correlate with the list at the top. It is also important to remember that this method can be used with all your students by varying the questions based on their proficiency level.

Use this page as a guide with the other example lessons by proficiency level. The other proficiency level examples are as follows:

- Early Intermediate Level (Beginning)
- Intermediate Level (Developing)
- Early Advanced Level (Expanding)
- Advanced Level (Bridging)

Example Lesson by Proficiency Level

Beginning Level (Entering)

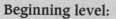

Beginning level:
- minimal comprehension
- no verbal production

Students are able to:
- listen
- draw
- mime
- point
- circle

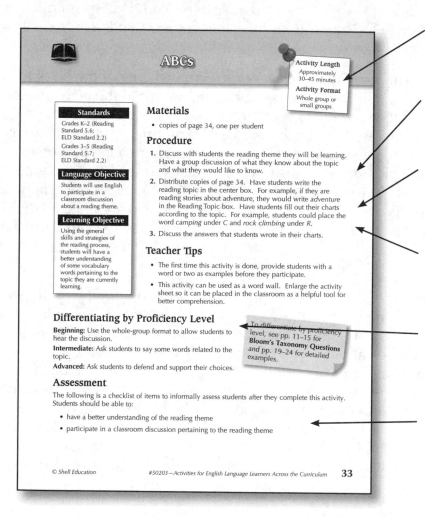

Use the whole-group format to allow students to hear the discussion.

Encourage students to draw their responses. Show students how to label their pictures in English.

Create a model of the ABC chart, either on chart paper or a transparency. Complete the chart as a group.

Allow students to respond in their first languages. Guide them in adding these responses to the chart in English.

Help students build their vocabulary by adding labeled pictures or drawings to any empty boxes on the chart.

As students share their answers, encourage students to come up to the chart and point to the words.

To guide this lesson with questioning, refer back to New Bloom's Taxonomy Questions by Levels of Proficiency (Beginning Level) on page 11. Here are some example questions:

Remembering: What is…?

Understanding: What is the main idea…?

Applying: What examples do you see…?

Analyzing: What are the parts of…?

Evaluating: What is another way you could…?

Creating: What would be different if…?

Example Lesson by Proficiency Level *(cont.)*

Early Intermediate Level (Beginning)

Early Intermediate Level:
- limited comprehension
- short spoken phrases

Students are able to:
- match
- choose
- act/act out
- move
- select

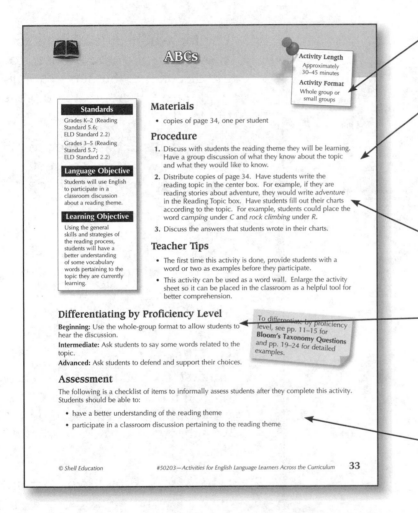

Use the whole-group format to allow students to hear the discussion.

Have several pictures pertaining to the topic. Also, have pictures of items not pertaining to the topic. Have students sort out the pictures to see the connection and to enhance comprehension.

Create a model of the ABC chart, either on chart paper or a transparency. Complete the chart as a group.

Write the words on 3"x 5" lined index cards. Have students match the word with the picture and then take both the word and picture to the chart and physically show where it should be placed.

Have students describe why the word belongs in the box.

To guide this lesson with questioning, refer back to New Bloom's Taxonomy Questions by Levels of Proficiency (Early Intermediate Level) on page 12. Here are some example questions:

Remembering: Can you choose…? Show me.

Applying: What examples can you find to…?

Evaluating: Would it be better if…? Why or why not?

Understanding: What can you say about…?

Analyzing: How is…related to…?

Creating: Suppose youcould… what would you do…?

Example Lesson by Proficiency Level *(cont.)*

Intermediate Level (Developing)

Intermediate Level:
- increased comprehension
- simple sentences

Students are able to:
- name
- categorize
- list
- label
- tell/say
- respond with phrases or sentences

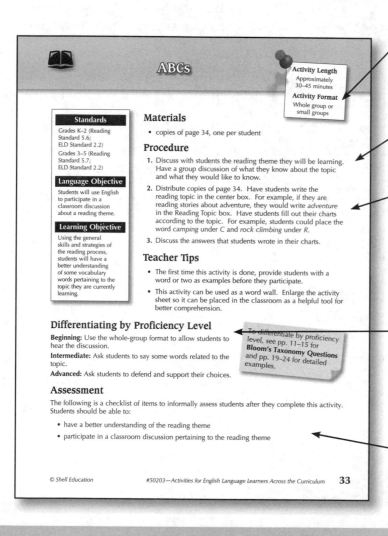

Use the whole-group format to allow students to be exposed to the discussion. Students can also work in small groups to help each other with comprehension.

Ask students to name the topic and some words that come to mind when they hear the topic.

Have students work in small groups. Distribute numerous 3"x 5" lined index cards with words on them. Allow students to work as a whole group to categorize the words and to integrate them on the chart.

Since students can follow multi-step directions, have them draw a picture pertaining to the topic, label the picture, and state why they chose to draw what they did.

Have students retell why certain answers were selected.

To guide this lesson with questioning, refer back to New Bloom's Taxonomy Questions by Levels of Proficiency (Intermediate Level) on page 13. Here are some example questions:

Remembering: Why did…?

Understanding: Which is the best answer…?

Applying: How would you use…?

Analyzing: What evidence can you find…?

Evaluating: How would you prove…? Disprove?

Creating: What would happen if…?

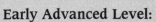

Example Lesson by Proficiency Level *(cont.)*

Early Advanced Level (Expanding)

Early Advanced Level:
- very good comprehension
- some errors in speech

Students are able to:
- role-play
- describe
- retell
- compare/contrast
- explain
- recall

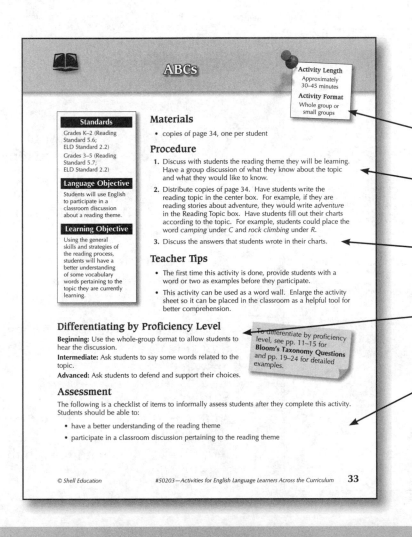

At this proficiency level, the activity format is your discretion.

Compare and contrast various ABC charts you have completed as a class.

Students can orally describe what they think the word means.

State a word pertaining to the topic out loud. Ask students to explain where it would belong on the chart.

Ask students to give you a definition of each of the words in their own words.

To guide this lesson with questioning, refer back to New Bloom's Taxonomy Questions by Levels of Proficiency (Early Advanced Level) on page 14. Here are some example questions:

Remembering: How would you explain…?

Applying: What approach would you use to…?

Evaluating: Would it be better if…?

Understanding: How would you summarize…?

Analyzing: What conclusions can you draw…?

Creating: What is an original way for the…?

Example Lesson by Proficiency Level (cont.)

Advanced Level (Bridging)

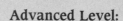

Advanced Level:
- comprehension comparable to native-English speakers
- speaks using complex sentences

Students are able to:
- justify
- defend
- support
- create
- analyze
- complete
- evaluate

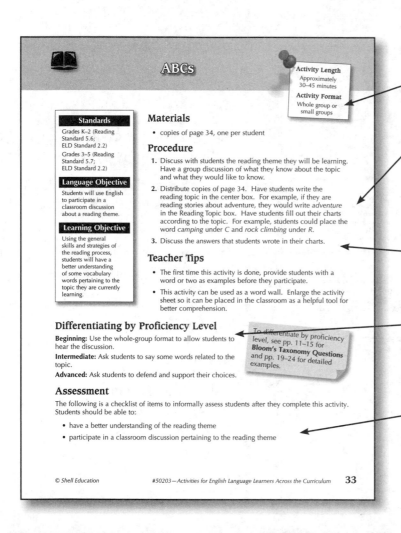

At this proficiency level, the activity format is at your discretion.

Present students with a list of words (some relevant to the topic and some not). Ask students which words belong in the chart. Encourage them to defend and support their choice.

Students can create sentences with their words as a form of comprehension.

Incorporate a written assignment for students to justify their answers.

Students can write a short summary of a conclusion they drew from the discussion. Their writing can be placed next to the word wall.

To guide this lesson with questioning, refer back to New Bloom's Taxonomy Questions by Levels of Proficiency (Advanced Level) on page 15. Here are some example questions:

Remembering: Which events show…?

Applying: How would you use…?

Evaluating: How would you have advised…?

Understanding: Why did…?

Analyzing: What clues led you to infer…?

Creating: What is an alternative plan if…?

Standards Correlations

Shell Education is committed to producing educational materials that are research and standards based. In this effort, we have correlated all of our products to the academic standards of all 50 states, the District of Columbia, and the Department of Defense Dependent Schools.

How to Find Standards Correlations

To print a customized correlation report of this product for your state, visit our website at **http://www.shelleducation.com** and follow the on-screen directions. If you require assistance in printing correlation reports, please contact Customer Service at 1-877-777-3450.

Purpose and Intent of Standards

The No Child Left Behind legislation mandates that all states adopt academic standards that identify the skills students will learn in kindergarten through grade twelve. While many states had already adopted academic standards prior to NCLB, the legislation set requirements to ensure the standards were detailed and comprehensive.

Standards are designed to focus instruction and guide adoption of curricula. Standards are statements that describe the criteria necessary for students to meet specific academic goals. They define the knowledge, skills, and content students should acquire at each level. Standards are also used to develop standardized tests to evaluate students' academic progress.

Teachers are required to demonstrate how their lessons meet state standards. State standards are used in development of all of our products, so educators can be assured they meet the academic requirements of each state.

McREL Compendium

We use the Mid-continent Research for Education and Learning (McREL) Compendium to create standards correlations. Each year, McREL analyzes state standards and revises the compendium. By following this procedure, McREL is able to produce a general compilation of national standards. Each lesson in this product is based on one or more McREL standards. The chart on the following pages lists each standard taught in this product and the page numbers for the corresponding lessons.

Correlation to TESOL Standards

The main focus of the activities in this book is to promote language development. The standards listed below support the language objectives presented throughout the activities.

Language Objectives	Page
2.1—To use English to achieve academically in all content areas: Students will use English to interact in the classroom. (K–5)	46, 67, 75, 77, 80, 81, 97, 103
2.2—To use English to achieve academically in all content areas: Students will use English to obtain, process, construct, and provide subject matter information in spoken and written form. (K–5)	33, 35, 37, 39, 41, 42, 43, 44, 48, 50, 52, 54, 55, 56, 58, 59, 60, 62, 63, 64, 65, 73, 78, 83, 85, 86, 88, 89, 91, 92, 95, 98, 100, 102, 104, 106, 108, 109, 110, 112, 115, 117, 118, 119, 120, 122, 123, 126, 128
2.3—To use English to achieve academically in all content areas: Students will use appropriate learning strategies to construct and apply academic knowledge. (K–5)	36, 71
3.1—To use English in socially and culturally appropriate ways: Students will use the appropriate language variety, register, and genre according to audience, purpose, and setting. (K–5)	69, 124

Correlation to McREL Standards

The main focus of the activities presented throughout the book is to promote language development. The standards listed below support the curriculum objectives presented throughout the activities.

Reading Objectives	Page
4.1—Generates questions about topics of personal interest (K–2)	44
4.2—Uses a variety of sources to gather information (K–2)	44
5.1—Uses mental images based on pictures and print to aid in comprehension text (K–2)	50
5.2—Uses meaning clues to aid comprehension and make predictions about content (K–2)	50
5.2—Establishes a purpose for reading (3–5)	44
5.3—Uses basic elements of phonetic analysis to decode unknown words (K–2)	36
5.4—Uses phonetic, structural analysis techniques, syntactic structure, and semantic context to decode unknown words (K–5)	36, 50
5.6—Understands level-appropriate sight words and vocabulary (K–2)	33, 39, 46, 48
5.7—Understands level-appropriate reading vocabulary (3–5)	33, 39, 46, 48
6.1—Uses reading skills and strategies to understand a variety of literary passages and texts (K–5)	42
6.2—Knows the defining characteristics of familiar genres (K–5)	42
6.3—Knows setting, main characters, main events, sequence, and problems in stories (K–2)	43
7.1—Uses reading skills and strategies to understand a variety of informational texts (K–2)	37
7.3—Summarizes information found in texts (K–2)	35, 43
7.3 Uses text organizers to determine the main ideas and to locate information in a text (3–5)	37
7.5—Summarizes and paraphrases information in texts (3–5)	35, 43
9.1—Understands the main idea or message in visual media (K–2)	41
10.3—Understands that there are common conventions used in media (K–2)	41
10.4—Understands that media messages and products are composed of a series of separate elements (3–5)	41

Correlation to McREL Standards *(cont.)*

Writing Objectives	Page
1.1—Prewriting: Uses prewriting strategies to plan written work (K–5)	52, 62, 63, 64, 65, 73
1.2—Drafting and Revising: Uses strategies to draft and revise written work (K–5)	52, 60, 62, 63, 64, 65, 73
1.3—Editing and Publishing: Uses strategies to edit and publish written work (K–5)	62, 63, 64, 65, 71, 73
1.4—Evaluates own and others' writing (K–5)	62, 63, 64, 65, 71, 73
1.5—Uses strategies to organize written work (K–2)	62, 63, 64, 65, 71, 73
1.5—Uses strategies to write for different audiences (3–5)	62, 63, 64, 65, 71, 73
1.6—Uses writing and other methods to describe familiar persons, places, objects, or experiences (K–2)	62, 63, 64, 65, 73
1.6—Uses strategies to write for a variety of purposes (3–5)	59, 62, 63, 64, 65, 73
1.7—Writes in a variety of forms or genres (K–2)	63, 73
1.7—Writes expository compositions (3–5)	63, 73
1.8—Writes for different purposes (K–2)	59, 63, 73
2.1—Uses descriptive words to convey basic ideas (K–2)	58, 67
2.1—Uses descriptive language that clarifies and enhances ideas (3–5)	58, 60, 67
3.2—Uses pronouns in written compositions (3–5)	58
3.3—Uses nouns in written compositions (K–5)	58
3.4—Uses verbs in written compositions (K–5)	58
3.5—Uses adjectives in written compositions (K–5)	56, 58
3.6—Uses adverbs in written compositions (K–5)	58
3.9—Uses conventions of spelling in written compositions (3–5)	54, 55
5.4—Uses basic elements of structural analysis to decode unknown words (K–2)	54, 55
8.1—Makes contributions in class and group discussions (K–5)	52
8.2—Asks and responds to questions (K–5)	52
8.5—Uses level-appropriate vocabulary in speech (K–2)	69
8.6—Uses level-appropriate vocabulary in speech (3–5)	69

Correlation to McREL Standards (cont.)

Mathematics Objectives	Page
1.1—Draws pictures to represent problems (K–2)	86
1.1—Uses a variety of strategies to understand problem situations (3–5)	86, 88, 89, 91, 92
1.2—Uses discussions with teachers and other students to understand problems (K–2)	80, 86, 88, 89, 91
1.2—Represents problems situations in a variety of forms (3–5)	81, 85, 86, 88
1.3—Explains to others how she or he went about solving a numerical problem (K–2)	86, 88
1.3 Understands that some ways of representing a problem are more helpful than others (3–5)	78, 80, 86, 91, 92
1.4—Makes organized lists or tables of information necessary for solving a problem (K–2)	78, 81, 86
1.4—Uses trial and error and the process of elimination to solve problems (3–5)	80, 86
1.7—Uses explanations of the methods and reasoning behind the problem solution to determine reasonableness of and to verify results with respect to the original problem (3–5)	80
2.1—Understands that numerals are symbols used to represent quantities or attributes of real-world objects (K–2)	91
2.2—Counts whole numbers (K–2)	77
2.2—Understands equivalent forms of basic percents, fractions, and decimals (3–5)	75
2.4—Understands basic whole number relationships (K–2)	81, 85
2.5—Understands the concept of a unit and its subdivision into equal parts (K–2)	75
4.2—Understands the concept of time and how it is measured (K–2)	92
4.3—Knows processes for telling time, counting money, and measuring length, weight, and temperature, using basic standard and non-standard units (K–2)	92
6.1—Collects and represents information about objects or events in simple graphs (K–2)	83
6.1—Understands that data represent specific pieces of information about real-world objects or activities (3–5)	83, 91
6.2—Understands that one can find out about a group of things by studying just a few of them (K–2)	83
9.1—Understands that numbers and the operations performed on them can be used to describe things in the real world and predict what might occur (3–5)	77

Correlation to McREL Standards *(cont.)*

Science Objectives	Page
1.0—Understands atmospheric processes and the water cycle (K–5)	95
3.0—Understands the composition and structure of the universe and the Earth's place in it (K–5)	95, 97
4.1—Knows that plants and animals closely resemble their parents (K–2)	98
4.1—Knows that many characteristics of plants and animals are inherited from its parents (3–5)	98
4.2—Knows that differences exist among individuals of the same kind of plant or animal (K–2)	98
5.0—Understands the structure and function of cells and organisms (K–5)	98
5.2—Knows that plants and animals have features that help them live in different environments (K–2)	100
5.2—Knows that living organisms have distinct structures and body systems that serve specific functions in growth, survival, and reproduction (3–5)	100
7.1—Knows that some kinds of organisms that once lived on Earth have completely disappeared (K–2)	102, 103, 106
7.1—Knows that fossils can be compared to one another and to living organisms to observe their similarities and differences (3–5)	102, 103, 106
7.2—Knows that there are similarities and differences in the appearance and behavior of plants and animals (K–2)	104
7.2—Knows different ways in which living things can be grouped (3–5)	104
11.2—Knows that good scientific explanations are based on evidence and scientific knowledge (3–5)	102, 103, 104, 106, 108, 109, 110, 112
12.1—Knows that scientific investigations involve asking and answering a question and comparing the answer to what scientists already know about the world (3–5)	97
12.2—Knows that scientists use different kinds of investigations depending on the questions they are trying to answer (3–5)	95, 98
13.1—Knows that in science it is helpful to work with a team and share findings with others (K–2)	95, 97, 98, 102, 103, 104, 106, 108, 109, 110, 112

Correlation to McREL Standards (cont.)

Social Studies Objectives	Page
1.3—Knows the cultural similarities and differences in clothes, homes, food, communication, technology, and cultural traditions between families now and in the past (K–2)	118
1.3—Understands daily life of a farm family from long ago (3–4)	118
2.1—Knows the location of school, home, neighborhood, community, state, and country (K–2)	120, 128
2.1—Knows major physical and human features of places as they are represented on maps and globes (3–5)	120
2.3—Knows the approximate location of major continents, mountain ranges, and bodies of water on Earth (3–5)	128
3.0—Understands the people, events, problems, and ideas that were significant in creating the history of their state (K–4)	123
3.1—Knows common ways in which rules and laws can be used (3–5)	126
3.6—Knows that a good rule or law solves a specific problem, is fair, and "does not go too far" (K–2)	126
4.2—Understands how individuals have worked to achieve the liberties and equality promised in the principles of American democracy and to improve the lives of people from many groups (K–2)	117
4.3—Understands how people over the last 200 years have continued to struggle to bring to all groups in American society the liberties and equality promised in the basic principles of American democracy (3–4)	117
4.5—Understands how important figures reacted to their times and why they were significant to the history of our democracy (K–2)	117
4.6—Understands the ways in which people in a variety of fields have advanced the cause of human rights, equality, and the common good (K–2)	117
4.7—Understands the reasons that Americans celebrate certain national holidays (K–2)	117
4.8—Knows the history of American symbols (K–2)	122
4.11—Understands how songs, symbols, and slogans demonstrate freedom of expression and the role of protest in a democracy (3–4)	122
5.1—Knows areas that can be classified as regions according to physical criteria (K–2)	115
5.1—Knows the characteristics of a variety of regions (3–5)	115
7.1—Understands the main ideas found in folktales, stories of great heroism, fables, legends, and myths from around the world that reflect the beliefs and ways of living of various cultures in times past (K-2)	119
7.5—Knows significant historical achievements of various cultures of the world (3–4)	119
8.5—Knows various systems of long-distance communication and their effects (K–2)	124

Reading

This page is to keep a record of when the activities were taught and what adjustments or modifications were made. This log can be used to keep track of students' progress, to make modifications, and for future planning.

Activities	Notes
ABCs	
A Live Book Report	
Circle Spelling	
Fill in the Squares	
Bright Idea	
Dissect a Newspaper	
Performing Fairy Tales	
Sequenced Bookmarks	
Study an Author	
Three in a Row	
Tricky Word Flags	
What's the Title?	

ABCs

Activity Length
Approximately 30–45 minutes

Activity Format
Whole group or small groups

Standards

Grades K–2 (Reading Standard 5.6; ELD Standard 2.2)

Grades 3–5 (Reading Standard 5.7; ELD Standard 2.2)

Language Objective

Students will use English to participate in a classroom discussion about a reading theme.

Learning Objective

Using the general skills and strategies of the reading process, students will have a better understanding of some vocabulary words pertaining to the topic they are currently learning.

Materials

- copies of page 34, one per student

Procedure

1. Discuss with students the reading theme they will be learning. Have a group discussion of what they know about the topic and what they would like to know.

2. Distribute copies of page 34. Have students write the reading topic in the center box. For example, if they are reading stories about adventure, they would write *adventure* in the Reading Topic box. Have students fill out their charts according to the topic. For example, students could place the word *camping* under *C* and *rock climbing* under *R*.

3. Discuss the answers that students wrote in their charts.

Teacher Tips

- The first time this activity is done, provide students with a word or two as examples before they participate.

- This activity can be used as a word wall. Enlarge the activity sheet so it can be placed in the classroom as a helpful tool for better comprehension.

Differentiating by Proficiency Level

Beginning: Use the whole-group format to allow students to hear the discussion.

Intermediate: Ask students to say some words related to the topic.

Advanced: Ask students to defend and support their choices.

To differentiate by proficiency level, see pp. 11–15 for **Bloom's Taxonomy Questions** and pp. 19–24 for detailed examples.

Assessment

The following is a checklist of items to informally assess students after they complete this activity. Students should be able to:

- have a better understanding of the reading theme

- participate in a classroom discussion pertaining to the reading theme

Name: _____ Date: _____

ABCs

Directions: Think about the reading topic. Write the reading topic in the center box. Fill in the other boxes with words that start with the letter shown in each box.

A	B	C
D	**E**	**F**
G	**Reading Topic**	**H**
I		**J**
K		**L**
M		**N**
O	**P**	**Q**
R	**S**	**T**
U	**V**	**W**
X	**Y**	**Z**

A Live Book Report

Activity Length
Approximately
45 minutes

Activity Format
Whole group and
small groups, or
partners

Standards

Grades K–2 (Reading
Standard 7.3;
ELD Standard 2.2)

Grades 3–5 (Reading
Standard 7.5;
ELD Standard 2.2)

Language Objective

Students will use spoken
English to create a book
report.

Learning Objective

Students will be able to
summarize information
found in text by giving a
creative oral presentation.

Materials

- students need props for their book reports,
  depending on the book

Procedure

1. Tell students they will be creating a live book report.
   Students should come up with a creative way to summarize
   and describe their books orally to the rest of the class. For
   example, students can create a poster, recite their favorite part,
   or create a song. Students should use props as part of their
   presentations.

2. As each book report is presented, encourage the rest of the
   class to be a good audience and afterward, share what they
   enjoyed most about the presentation.

Teacher Tips

- The first time you do this, have students work with partners or
  in small groups to prepare and present.

- Offer suggestions for students who are having a difficult time
  coming up with ideas for their book report.

Differentiating by Proficiency Level

Beginning: Encourage students to draw their responses.

Intermediate: Encourage students to answer in complete
sentences.

Advanced: Ask students to paraphrase what they read.

To differentiate by proficiency
level, see pp. 11–15 for
Bloom's Taxonomy Questions
and pp. 19–24 for detailed
examples.

Assessment

The following is a checklist of items to informally assess students after they complete this activity.
Students should be able to:

- practice listening skills by listening to their classmates as they share book reports

- practice reading comprehension skills by summarizing their selected reading book

- orally summarize and/or describe their books

Circle Spelling

Activity Length
Approximately 15 minutes

Activity Format
Whole group or small group

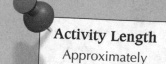

Standards

Grades K–2 (Reading Standard 5.3; ELD Standard 2.3)

Grades 3–5 (Reading Standard 5.4; ELD Standard 2.3)

Language Objective

Students will participate in an oral spelling game to improve spelling skills.

Learning Objective

Students will strengthen spelling skills by decoding unknown words using structural analysis techniques.

Materials

- teacher-prepared list of spelling words for review
- alphabet chart or poster for students' reference

Procedure

1. Ask students to stand up in a circle for a spelling review. Call out a spelling word and select one student to begin by giving the first letter of the word.

2. Have the student to the starter's left give the next letter of the word and continue the process, with one student giving each letter until all the letters of the word have been given.

3. After the last letter of the word has been given, students should chant, "Circle, circle, around the circle."

4. Call out another spelling word and repeat the process.

Teacher Tip

- As an extension, have students define the spelling words and use them in a sentence.

Differentiating by Proficiency Level

Beginning: Ask students to point to the letters as they say them.

Intermediate: Ask students to say the definition of the word.

Advanced: Ask students to respond in writing using small writing boards.

To differentiate by proficiency level, see pp. 11–15 for **Bloom's Taxonomy Questions** and pp. 19–24 for detailed examples.

Assessment

The following is a checklist of items to informally assess students after they complete this activity. Students should be able to:

- practice listening skills by listening to their classmates as they spell level-appropriate words
- practice spelling level-appropriate words

Fill in the Squares

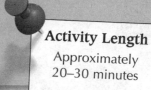

Activity Length
Approximately
20–30 minutes

Activity Format
Small groups or
partners

Standards

Grades K–2 (Reading Standard 7.1; ELD Standard 2.2)

Grades 3–5 (Reading Standard 7.3; ELD Standard 2.2)

Language Objective

Students will use English to select, connect, and explain information about a reading topic.

Learning Objective

Students will be able to build comprehension by using reading skills and strategies as a guide in completing a text organizer.

Materials

- copies of page 38, one per student

Procedure

1. Divide students into pairs or small groups. Distribute copies of page 38.

2. Explain the activity to students. Tell students to write across the top of the chart the three categories you give them.

3. On the left side of the paper in the shaded boxes, students should fill in the boxes with letters you also provide.

4. Students complete the page by writing one word in each box that matches the category word on top and begins with the letters along the side. For example, if you are reading stories about courage, a category word you could select is *hero*. The students would be asked to write the word *hero* in one of the shaded boxes on the top. If you selected the letter *M* as one of the letters to be written in the left column, students could write *Martin Luther King Jr.* in the box that matches the category word on top and begins with the letter *M*.

5. Discuss the answers that students wrote on their papers.

Teacher Tip

- Make sure you do an example with all of your students before you start the activity.

Differentiating by Proficiency Level

Beginning: Encourage students to draw their responses and show students how to label their pictures in English.

Intermediate: Have students work in small groups to discuss answers.

Advanced: Encourage students to use more complex content vocabulary.

To differentiate by proficiency level, see pp. 11–15 for **Bloom's Taxonomy Questions** and pp. 19–24 for detailed examples.

Assessment

The following is a checklist of items to informally assess students after they complete this activity. Students should be able to:

- participate in classroom discussion pertaining to the reading theme
- practice comprehension skills by correctly filling out the activity page

Name: _____   Date: _____

Fill in the Squares

Directions: Write the three categories your teacher tells you to write on the top row of boxes. Fill in the boxes along the left side with the letters your teacher tells you to write. Complete the page by writing one word in each box that matches the category word on the top and begins with the letters along the side.

Bright Idea

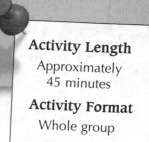

Activity Length
Approximately
45 minutes

Activity Format
Whole group

Standards

Grades K–2 (Reading
Standard 5.6;
ELD Standard 2.2)

Grades 3–5 (Reading
Standard 5.7;
ELD Standard 2.2)

Language Objective

Students will use English
to make personal
connections among
vocabulary words.

Learning Objective

Students will be able to
take a list of vocabulary
words they are currently
studying and create
various personal
associations.

Materials

- teacher-prepared list of vocabulary words currently being studied, displayed for the class to see
- sheets of construction paper, with word associations written on them (see examples below)
- copies of page 40, one copy for every two students (cut in half)
- scissors for each student

Procedure

1. Write word associations on each sheet of construction paper (e.g., *synonym*, *contraction*, *verb*, *noun*, *antonym*, *adjective*) and hang the sheets of paper around the classroom.

2. Distribute copies of page 40 to students and have them cut out their lightbulbs, so each student has one.

3. Have students select one vocabulary word from the displayed list and write that word on their lightbulb.

4. Explain that when you say, "Make an association!" every student is to choose a category that their word belongs to.

5. Have students explain their associations. For example, if a student chooses synonym, they need to explain how their word can be a synonym for another word and state that word.

Teacher Tip

- It is possible that a student will make more than one association with a vocabulary word.

Differentiating by Proficiency Level

Beginning: Provide choices for completing word associations.

Intermediate: Have students work as a group to categorize their word associations.

Advanced: Encourage students to use more complex content vocabulary when explaining their word associations.

To differentiate by proficiency level, see pp. 11–15 for **Bloom's Taxonomy Questions** and pp. 19–24 for detailed examples.

Assessment

The following is a checklist of items to informally assess students after they complete this activity. Students should be able to:

- make personal associations among vocabulary words

Bright Idea

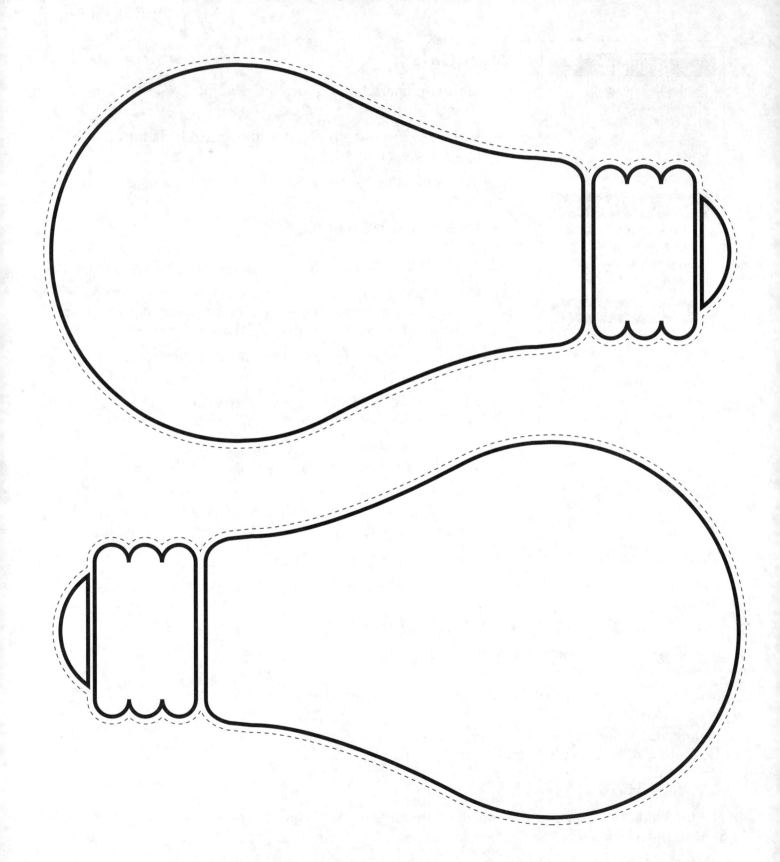

Dissect a Newspaper

Activity Length
Approximately
45 minutes

Activity Format
Whole group and
small groups

Standards

Grades K–2 (Reading Standards 9.1, 10.3; ELD Standard 2.2)

Grades 3–5 (Reading Standard 10.4; ELD Standard 2.2)

Language Objective

Students will use oral and written English to obtain, process, and provide information about newspapers.

Learning Objective

Students will be able to understand the different components of a newspaper by reading and describing the different sections.

Materials

- a variety of newspapers (two or three per group of students)
- 3"x 5" lined index cards (five per group)

Procedure

1. Tell students they will be learning about the newspaper. Ask the class questions about the newspaper, like "What can you learn from a newspaper?" and "What's your favorite part of the newspaper?"

2. Divide the class into groups of five. Distribute index cards to each group.

3. Give each group several newspapers to study and dissect. In their groups, each member should write a short description on their index card of the section he or she read. For example, if a student is reading the local section, he or she might write that this section only covers stories of the state they live in.

4. Each group will select two representatives to read different sections of the newspaper to the rest of the class. The class will decide which section the student is reading from.

Teacher Tip

- As an extended activity, have the class work together to write a class newspaper.

Differentiating by Proficiency Level

Beginning: Give students a simple sentence frame to complete.

Intermediate: Encourage students to tell more about their answers.

Advanced: Encourage students to use academic language in their oral responses.

> To differentiate by proficiency level, see pp. 11–15 for **Bloom's Taxonomy Questions** and pp. 19–24 for detailed examples.

Assessment

The following is a checklist of items to informally assess students after they complete this activity. Students should be able to:

- describe the sections of a newspaper
- practice socialization skills by discussing with classmates the various sections of a newspaper
- distinguish between the different sections of the newspaper
- practice reading comprehension skills by summarizing sections of a newspaper

Performing Fairy Tales

Activity Length
Approximately
45 minutes

Activity Format
Whole group and
small groups

Standards

Grades K–2 (Reading Standards 6.1, 6.2; ELD Standard 2.2)

Grades 3–5 (Reading Standards 6.1, 6.2; ELD Standard 2.2)

Language Objective

Students will work in groups to read and perform different versions of a fairy tale. Then students will use English to compare and contrast the different versions.

Learning Objective

Students will have a better understanding of a variety of fairy tale passages by defining similarities and differences.

Materials

- several different versions of the same fairy tales or stories
- chart paper

Procedure

1. Collect several different versions of the same fairy tale or story (such as *Cinderella*, *The Three Little Pigs*, *Rumplestilskin*, etc.).

2. Divide the class into groups. Each group will read one version of the story. After they are done reading, have students plan how to act out the story in front of the class.

3. When all groups are ready, have each group perform its version of the story.

4. After all groups have performed, lead a class discussion on how different versions of the fairy tales or stories were similar and different.

5. Write a list of these similarities and differences on chart paper.

Teacher Tip

- For students who are shy or scared to act in front of their classmates, assign the role of the narrator to them.

Differentiating by Proficiency Level

Beginning: Allow students to act out their responses during the discussion.

Intermediate: Have students work in small groups to discuss answers.

Advanced: Ask students to draw conclusions about the topic.

To differentiate by proficiency level, see pp. 11–15 for **Bloom's Taxonomy Questions** and pp. 19–24 for detailed examples.

Assessment

The following is a checklist of items to informally assess students after they complete this activity. Students should be able to:

- practice oral presentation skills by performing different versions of fairy tales
- distinguish between similarities and differences
- work cooperatively
- participate in a classroom discussion pertaining to the different versions of the same stories

Sequenced Bookmarks

Activity Length
Approximately 30–45 minutes

Activity Format
Whole class, each student working independently, then partners

Standards

Grades K–2 (Reading Standards 6.3, 7.3; ELD Standard 2.2)

Grades 3–5 (Reading Standard 7.5; ELD Standard 2.2)

Language Objective

Students will use English to retell the sequence of events of a story.

Learning Objective

Students will be able to develop sequencing skills by retelling a story in sequential order.

Materials

- storybooks for students to read
- strips of paper for creating bookmarks, divided into three sections
- crayons or markers for each student

Procedure

1. Have students read storybooks appropriate to their proficiency levels. For students who are not independent readers, you may read a story aloud to them.

2. After reading a story, each student must create a bookmark on their strip of paper to show the beginning, the middle, and the ending.

3. Students select partners and give a summary of the book they read using the bookmark as a guide. Bookmarks may be left inside books so future readers can use them as a "sneak preview."

Teacher Tips

- The first time you use this activity, create a class bookmark, by soliciting students' ideas and drawing the bookmark on chart paper or on the board so that all students can see the beginning, the middle, and the ending.

- Wordless books are a great way to help students with creativity. It allows them to think about the pictures and say what they think is happening.

Differentiating by Proficiency Level

Beginning: Add labeled pictures or drawings to the bookmarks.

Intermediate: Ask students to label their pictures/drawings.

Advanced: Ask students to summarize their learning with complete sentences.

To differentiate by proficiency level, see pp. 11–15 for **Bloom's Taxonomy Questions** and pp. 19–24 for detailed examples.

Assessment

The following is a checklist of items to informally assess students after they complete this activity. Students should be able to:

- correctly sequence their bookmarks based on the story they selected

Study an Author

Standards

Grades K–2 (Reading Standards 4.1, 4.2; ELD Standard 2.2)

Grades 3–5 (Reading Standard 5.2; ELD Standard 2.2)

Language Objective

Students will compare and contrast two works by an author.

Learning Objective

Students will learn about authors by using reading skills and strategies to understand a variety of informational texts.

Materials

- multiple copies of two different books written by the same author
- copies of page 45, one per pair of students

Procedure

1. Ask students what an author is (someone who writes books, stories, poems, etc.).

2. Tell students that they will work in pairs to compare and contrast two books written by the same author. Have students read both books with their partners.

3. Distribute copies of page 45. Tell students to write the name of their author on their paper. In the left circle, tell students to write the name of the book title and facts of how that book is different from the other book. In the right circle, tell students to write the name of the other book title and facts of how that book is different from the other book. In the middle, where the circles overlap, tell students to write how both books are similar. Give students time to read their books with their partners.

4. Have students share their facts with the class.

Teacher Tips

- Make sure students understand how to complete the graphic organizer.
- Pair a lower-level proficiency student and a higher-level proficiency student.

Differentiating by Proficiency Level

Beginning: Encourage students to draw their responses.

Intermediate: Have students explain their answers.

Advanced: Ask students to paraphrase what they learned.

To differentiate by proficiency level, see pp. 11–15 for **Bloom's Taxonomy Questions** and pp. 19–24 for detailed examples.

Assessment

The following is a checklist of items to informally assess students after they complete this activity. Students should be able to:

- tell some facts about their selected books
- work cooperatively on gathering facts
- develop oral presentation skills by sharing facts about their selected books

Name: _____   Date: _____

Study an Author

Directions: Write the name of your author on the line. In the left circle, write the title of one book and five ways that book is different from the second book. In the right circle, write the title of the other book and five ways that book is different from the first book. In the middle, where the circles overlap, write three ways the two books are similar.

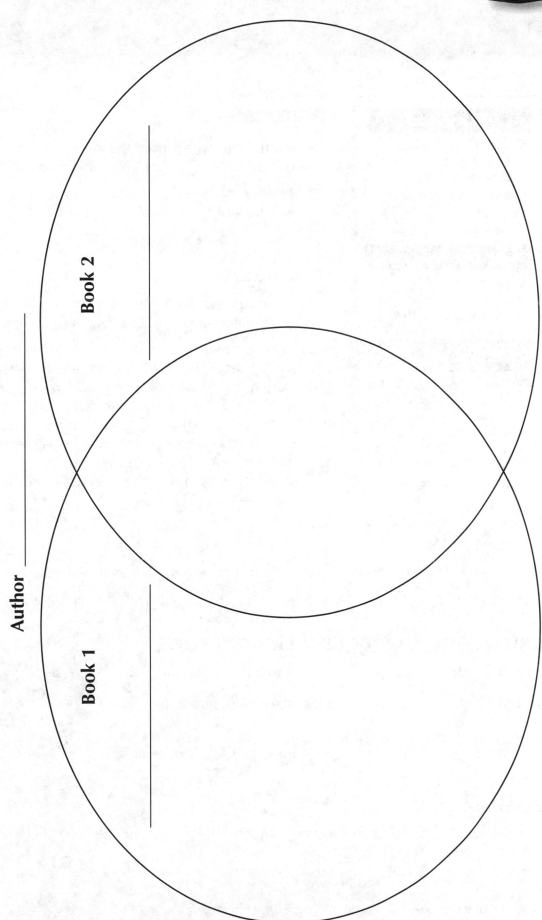

Author

Book 1

Book 2

Three in a Row

Activity Length
Approximately
45 minutes

Activity Format
Partners

Standards

Grades K–2 (Reading
Standard 5.6;
ELD Standard 2.1)

Grades 3–5 (Reading
Standard 5.7;
ELD Standard 2.1)

Language Objective

Students will use English
to practice vocabulary by
writing words and then
listening for clues about
them.

Learning Objective

Students will reinforce
their knowledge of newly
acquired vocabulary
terms by participating in a
traditional game.

Materials

- vocabulary words from the current reading passage or story, posted on chart paper or on the board

- teacher-prepared sentences—one sentence that shows the meaning of each vocabulary word without using the word

- copies of page 47, one per student

Procedure

1. Distribute copies of page 47. Have students work in pairs to write different vocabulary words in the squares.

2. Read a sentence to students and ask them to put an *X* in the square when the word matches the sentence. For example, if a student pair wrote the word *timid* in a square and the sentence read aloud was, "She was scared to speak because she was shy," the pair would place an *X* in that square. When a pair gets three *X*s in a row (horizontally, vertically, or diagonally), they call out, "Three in a row!" and read back the words. Have students explain why the selected words are correct for the sentences.

Teacher Tips

- As an extended activity, have students create new sentences with the vocabulary words.

- Have students draw a picture of each word to help with comprehension.

Differentiating by Proficiency Level

Beginning: Repeat key vocabulary words in a systematic way.

Intermediate: Encourage students to tell more about the words.

Advanced: Ask students to explain how their knowledge about the words has changed.

To differentiate by proficiency level, see pp. 11–15 for **Bloom's Taxonomy Questions** and pp. 19–24 for detailed examples.

Assessment

The following is a checklist of items to informally assess students after they complete this activity. Students should be able to:

- write selected vocabulary words

- recognize correct usage of vocabulary terms

Three in a Row

Directions: Fill in the boxes with the words your teacher gives you. Listen to the sentence. If the sentence tells about a word in a box, put an *X* in the box. When you get three *X*s in a row (horizontally, vertically, or diagonally), call out, "Three in a row!"

Tricky Word Flags

Activity Length
Approximately 30–45 minutes

Activity Format
Whole group or small groups

Standards

Grades K–2 (Reading Standard 5.6; ELD Standard 2.2)

Grades 3–5 (Reading Standard 5.7; ELD Standard 2.2)

Language Objective

Students will listen to a story read aloud in English and identify unfamiliar words.

Learning Objective

Students will be able to state the definitions of newly acquired vocabulary words by using a variety of context clues.

Materials

- copies of page 49, one for every six students
- craft sticks or straws, one per student
- scissors for each student

Procedure

1. Distribute one flag to each student. Have students prepare their own tricky word flags by gluing them to straws or craft sticks. Seat students so they can listen as you read a story aloud.

2. Tell students that you will read a book and they must listen to the story. If there are any words that they do not understand during the story, they must raise their tricky word flag.

3. Stop reading the story whenever a flag is raised. The student who raised the flag must ask the meaning of the unknown word. Share a student friendly definition or explanation of the word. After you finish reading the book, review the "tricky words" and their meanings.

Teacher Tip

- Students can find tricky words when they are reading independently. They can try to find the meanings of the unfamiliar words on their own using a simple dictionary or they can ask you the meanings as you circulate around the classroom during reading time.

Differentiating by Proficiency Level

Beginning: Use the whole-group format to allow students to hear the discussion.

Intermediate: Encourage students to answer in complete sentences.

Advanced: Ask students to paraphrase what they have learned.

To differentiate by proficiency level, see pp. 11–15 for **Bloom's Taxonomy Questions** and pp. 19–24 for detailed examples.

Assessment

The following is a checklist of items to informally assess students after they complete this activity. Students should be able to:

- listen to a story read aloud
- practice listening skills by identifying unfamiliar words in a story
- state the definitions of newly acquired vocabulary words

Tricky Word Flags

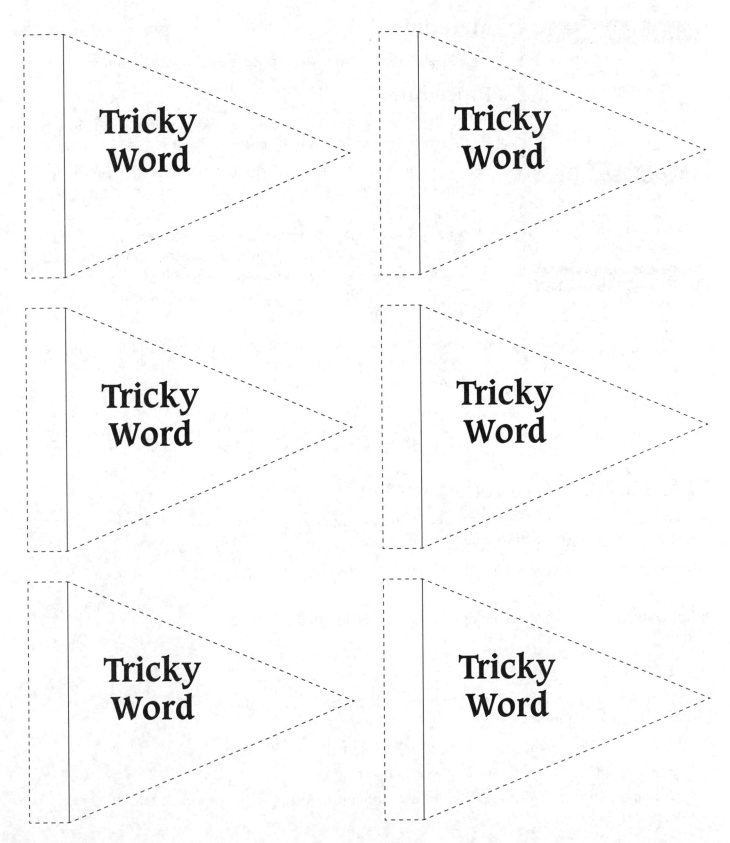

Tricky
Word

Tricky
Word

Tricky
Word

Tricky
Word

Tricky
Word

Tricky
Word

What's the Title?

Activity Length
Approximately
30 minutes

Activity Format
Whole group

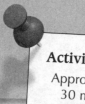

Standards

Grades K–2 (Reading Standards 5.1, 5.2; ELD Standard 2.2)

Grades 3–5 (Reading Standard 5.4; ELD Standard 2.2)

Language Objective

Students will listen to a short story or poem in English and then suggest appropriate titles.

Learning Objective

Students will be able to identify the main theme or topic of a story or poem and generate appropriate titles.

Materials

- variety of short stories and poems unfamiliar to students

Procedure

1. Tell students to listen carefully while you read a short story or poem to them. Do not tell students the title.

2. After you finish reading, ask students to think of appropriate titles for the story or poem and then write students' suggestions on the board.

3. After generating a list of possible titles, tell students the real title of the story or poem. Lead a discussion about why the author might have chosen that particular title.

Teacher Tips

- Reverse this activity by reading the true title of a story or poem to the class. Students should then generate ideas of what they think the story or poem is about.

- Try this same activity with students' own written stories and poems. Ideas generated and discussions about the titles will help students to carefully select a title for their writing piece.

Differentiating by Proficiency Level

Beginning: Allow students to first discuss in their native languages and then respond in English.

Intermediate: Encourage students to tell more about their answers.

Advanced: Ask students to create an alternative version of the activity.

To differentiate by proficiency level, see pp. 11–15 for **Bloom's Taxonomy Questions** and pp. 19–24 for detailed examples.

Assessment

The following is a checklist of items to informally assess students after they complete this activity. Students should be able to:

- practice listening skills as the story or poem is being read to them

- generate appropriate titles for stories and poems

- participate in a classroom discussion pertaining to selecting an appropriate title

Writing

This page is to keep a record of when the activities were taught and what adjustments or modifications were made. This log can be used to keep track of students' progress, to make modifications, and for future planning.

Activities	Notes
ABCs	
Acting Out Antonyms	
Action-Play Compound Word Story	
Name It!	
Brainstorming Blanks	
Category Race	
Change the Words	
Holiday Story Starters	
The Longest Sentence	
Object Stories	
So-Close Pictures	
The Fewest Clues	
Idiom Pictures	
Word Changes	
World's Longest Story	

ABCs

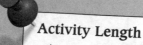

Activity Length
Approximately
30–45 minutes

Activity Format
Whole group or
small groups

Standards

Grades K–2 (Writing
Standards 1.2, 8.1, 8.2;
ELD Standard 2.2)

Grades 3–5 (Writing
Standard 1.1;
ELD Standard 2.2)

Language Objective

Students will use English
to participate in a
classroom discussion
about a writing theme.

Learning Objective

Students will be able to
use prewriting strategies,
such as a graphic
organizer to plan written
work.

Materials

- copies of page 53, one per student

Procedure

1. Discuss with students the writing theme they are focusing on in class. Have a group discussion of what they know about the theme and what they would like to know.

2. Distribute copies of page 53. Have students write the writing topic in the center box. For example, if they are writing stories with a family theme, they would write *family* in the Writing Topic box and they could fill in the chart according to the topic. The word *Mom* could be placed under *M*, the word *loving* under *L*, and so on.

3. Discuss the answers students wrote in their charts. Have students do a writing assignment that integrates the terms they have listed.

Teacher Tips

- The first time this activity is done, provide students with a word or two as examples before they participate.

- This activity can be used as a word wall. Enlarge the activity sheet so it can be placed in the classroom as a helpful tool for better comprehension.

Differentiating by Proficiency Level

Beginning: Use the whole-group format to allow students to hear the discussion.

Intermediate: Ask students to say some words related to the topic.

Advanced: Ask students to defend and support their choices.

To differentiate by proficiency level, see pp. 11–15 for **Bloom's Taxonomy Questions** and pp. 19–24 for detailed examples.

Assessment

The following is a checklist of items to informally assess students after they complete this activity. Students should be able to:

- have a better understanding of the writing theme

- participate in a classroom discussion pertaining to the writing theme

Name: _____   Date: _____

ABCs

Directions: Think about the writing topic. Write the writing topic in the center box. Fill in the other boxes with words that start with the letter shown in each box.

A	B	C
D	**E**	**F**
G	**Writing Topic**	**H**
I		**J**
K		**L**
M		**N**
O	**P**	**Q**
R	**S**	**T**
U	**V**	**W**
X	**Y**	**Z**

Acting Out Antonyms

Activity Length
Approximately 30 minutes

Activity Format
Partners, then whole group

Standards

Grades K–2 (Writing Standard 5.4; ELD Standard 2.2)

Grades 3–5 (Writing Standard 3.9; ELD Standard 2.2)

Language Objective

Students will work in pairs to select, connect, and act out antonyms.

Learning Objective

Students will have a better understanding of what an antonym is by role-playing words with opposite meanings.

Materials

- lined paper, one sheet for each student

Procedure

1. Discuss what *opposite* means by providing several examples, such as *tall/short*, *happy/sad*, and *hot/cold*. Tell students these opposites are called *antonyms*. Have students help create a list of antonyms. Write their responses on the board.

2. Have students work with a partner. Each pair of students must choose antonyms to act out for the rest of the class to guess. Students can think of their own antonyms or use the examples provided.

3. When everyone is ready, have pairs of students take turns acting out their antonyms. As students are performing their antonyms, students watching should write their guesses on their sheet of paper.

4. After each performance, the class should try to guess the antonym.

Teacher Tip

- Have pictures of various antonyms as visuals.

Differentiating by Proficiency Level

Beginning: Use the whole-group format to allow students to hear the discussion.

Intermediate: Ask students to say some words related to the topic.

Advanced: Ask students to defend and support their choices.

To differentiate by proficiency level, see pp. 11–15 for **Bloom's Taxonomy Questions** and pp. 19–24 for detailed examples.

Assessment

The following is a checklist of items to informally assess students after they complete this activity. Students should be able to:

- state what an antonym is
- participate in a classroom discussion by helping to create some antonym word pairs
- act out the meanings of antonyms

Action-Play Compound Word Story

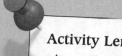

Activity Length
Approximately
45 minutes

Activity Format
Small groups, then
whole group

Standards

Grades K–2 (Writing
Standard 5.4;
ELD Standard 2.2)

Grades 3–5 (Writing
Standard 3.9;
ELD Standard 2.2)

Language Objective

Students will use
English to make a list
of compound words,
work in groups to write
a story with at least five
compound words, and
then act out the words.

Learning Objective

Students will have a
better understanding
of what a compound
word is by working
cooperatively to act out
a story that contains
compound words.

Materials

- lined paper, one sheet for each group
- timer

Procedure

1. Discuss what a compound word is (two words joined together to form one word). Give several examples, such as *snowman*, *potluck*, *notebook*, and *sunlight*.

2. Have students help create a list of compound words. Write their responses on the board. Tell students they will be working in groups to write a story that contains at least five compound words. When their stories are written, they will read their stories aloud and act out the compound words.

3. Divide the class into groups. Set the timer for 15 minutes and have each group work together to write their story.

4. Have groups decide on a way to portray their compound words as their story is read. For example, for the word *cowboy*, they could say, "Moo" and then point to a boy.

5. Have each group perform their stories that portray their compound words.

Teacher Tip

- Have students work in small groups to make up their own action play with compound words.

Differentiating by Proficiency Level

Beginning: Ask students to point to the compound words as they say them.

Intermediate: Give students multi-step directions to complete the activity.

Advanced: Provide complex language structures for students as models.

To differentiate by proficiency level, see pp. 11–15 for **Bloom's Taxonomy Questions** and pp. 19–24 for detailed examples.

Assessment

The following is a checklist of items to informally assess students after they complete this activity. Students should be able to:

- define what a compound word is
- write a short story that includes compound words

Name It!

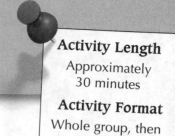

Activity Length
Approximately
30 minutes

Activity Format
Whole group, then
small group

Standards

Grades K–2 (Writing
Standard 3.5;
ELD Standard 2.2)

Grades 3–5 (Writing
Standard 3.5;
ELD Standard 2.2)

Language Objective

Students will use English
to list nouns that relate to
specific adjectives.

Learning Objective

Students will be able to
generate a list of items
in a specific category
or group based on the
adjective.

Materials

- timer
- copy of page 57 (cut up into individual strips and placed in a box or a jar)
- scratch paper, one sheet for each group

Procedure

1. Discuss the meaning of an *adjective* (a word that describes a noun). Read a few prompts from page 57 to the class. As a class, have students answer the prompts orally.

2. Divide the class into groups. Set the timer for 15 minutes. Have one person from each group get one slip of paper that has an adjective prompt.

3. One student reads the adjective prompt and the group brainstorms answers on a sheet of paper.

4. Have each group discuss its answers.

5. Ask another member of the group to get new slips of paper until the group has completed five adjective prompts.

Teacher Tip

- As the school year progresses, make your own list of adjectives prompts that have been taught in previous lessons.

Differentiating by Proficiency Level

Beginning: Provide students with specific examples of each adjective.

Intermediate: Encourage students to answer in complete sentences.

Advanced: Ask students to create their own examples of the activity.

To differentiate by proficiency level, see pp. 11–15 for **Bloom's Taxonomy Questions** and pp. 19–24 for detailed examples.

Assessment

The following is a checklist of items to informally assess students after they complete this activity. Students should be able to:

- state what an adjective is
- work cooperatively in groups to list adjective prompts

Name It!

Name eight things that are fast.	Name four things that are flexible.
Name three things that are slippery.	Name three things that are crusty.
Name six things that are hot.	Name four things that are scary.
Name six things that are slow.	Name three things that are squishy.
Name seven things that are cold.	Name two things that are woven.
Name five things that are sticky.	Name six things that are light.
Name nine things that are hard.	Name five things that are foldable.
Name eight things that are soft.	Name three things that are rotten.
Name seven things that are noisy.	Name four things that are fresh.
Name six things that are quiet.	Name three things that are sour.
Name four things that are sandy.	Name three things that are awkward.
Name two things that are expensive.	Name four things that are aromatic.
Name nine things that are tall.	Name three things that are colorful.

Brainstorming Blanks

Activity Length
Approximately
15 minutes

Activity Format
Whole group and
partners

Standards

Grades K–2 (Writing
Standards 2.1, 3.3–3.6;
ELD Standard 2.2)

Grades 3–5 (Writing
Standards 2.1, 3.2–3.6;
ELD Standard 2.2)

Language Objective

Students will use English
to complete sentence
frames in several ways.

Learning Objective

Students will work
cooperatively with a
partner to brainstorm
multiple answers that will
complete a statement.

Materials

- lined paper, one sheet per pair of students

Procedure

1. Write a sentence frame on the board, such as the following: *We can _____ at school every day.*

2. Read the sentence frame to the class. Have students think of a few words that would make sense in the blank (e.g., *play, read, slide, learn*). Write students' ideas on the board.

3. Divide the class into pairs. Write a new sentence frame on the board. Students must work with their partners to generate as many ideas as possible to fill in the blank. Students should make a list of these ideas on their sheet of paper.

4. Have students share their answers with the whole class.

5. Write all of the ideas on the board, showing the class how many ideas they generated.

Teacher Tips

- If you find students are having difficulties, stop and try a few more examples as a class.

- Encourage students to create their own statements for the class to use as examples.

Differentiating by Proficiency Level

Beginning: Encourage students to draw their responses.
Intermediate: Have students explain their answers.
Advanced: Encourage students to use more complex content vocabulary or to create more complex sentence frames.

To differentiate by proficiency level, see pp. 11–15 for **Bloom's Taxonomy Questions** and pp. 19–24 for detailed examples.

Assessment

The following is a checklist of items to informally assess students after they complete this activity. Students should be able to:

- work cooperatively in pairs to complete sentence frames

- brainstorm a list of numerous answers that correctly fill in the blank

Category Race

Standards

Grades K–2 (Writing Standard 1.8; ELD Standard 2.2)

Grades 3–5 (Writing Standard 1.6; ELD Standard 2.2)

Language Objective

Students will use English to list things that belong to a category.

Learning Objective

Students will work cooperatively with team members to help develop categorization skills.

Materials

- chart paper, one sheet for each group of students
- timer

Procedure

1. Divide the class into small groups. Give each group a sheet of chart paper.

2. Select a category, such as animals. Set the timer for five minutes. When you say, "Go," each group must write the names of as many animals as they can think of on their chart paper. For example, a group might write *dog*, *cat*, *pig*, *squirrel*, etc. Encourage students to confer with their teammates for ideas.

3. When the timer goes off, have students stop. Have groups read their answers aloud to the class. The team that has the most items listed wins.

Teacher Tip

- You might choose to use this activity to reinforce spelling skills and award an extra point for every word spelled correctly.

Differentiating by Proficiency Level

Beginning: Allow students to first discuss in their native languages and then respond in English.

Intermediate: Have students work in small groups to discuss answers.

Advanced: Ask students to create their own categories.

To differentiate by proficiency level, see pp. 11–15 for **Bloom's Taxonomy Questions** and pp. 19–24 for detailed examples.

Assessment

The following is a checklist of items to informally assess students after they complete this activity. Students should be able to:

- develop categorization skills
- state why the items within a given category are grouped together
- work cooperatively in small groups to generate a list of things that belong to a category

Change the Words

Activity Length
Approximately 30 minutes

Activity Format
Partners

Standards

Grades K–2 (Writing Standard 1.2; ELD Standard 2.2)

Grades 3–5 (Writing Standard 2.1; ELD Standard 2.2)

Language Objective

Students will follow written directions in English to change word spellings and create new words.

Learning Objective

Students will work with a partner in identifying new words by following a variety of context clues.

Materials

- copies of page 61, one per student (You may choose to modify this page from the Teacher Resource CD.)
- alphabet chart or poster for students' reference

Procedure

1. Distribute copies of page 61. Tell students to work with a partner to look at the words in capital letters at the top of each section.

2. Students will follow the directions underneath each capitalized word to change it to a different word.

3. After students have changed their words, have them compare their answers with a partner to see if they are correct.

Answer Key

CAT: 1. c, **2.** c, o, **3.** c, o, m, **4.** c, o, m, b **New word:** comb;
SAME: 1. r, **2.** r, o, **3.** r, o, __, k **4.** r, o, c, k **New word:** *rock*;
MITTEN: 1. __, ___, d, d, ___, ___, **2.** ___, ___, d, d, ___, e **3.** p, ___, d, d, ___, ___, e. **4.** p, u, d, d, ___, e,
5. p, u, d, d, l, e **New word:** puddle

Teacher Tip

- To extend the activity, when students have changed words, have them write a sentence with both the new word and the original word in it.

Differentiating by Proficiency Level

Beginning: Ask students to point to the letters as they say them.

Intermediate: Have students discuss the answer to each step with their partners.

Advanced: Ask students to create an alternative version of the activity.

To differentiate by proficiency level, see pp. 11–15 for **Bloom's Taxonomy Questions** and pp. 19–24 for detailed examples.

Assessment

The following is a checklist of items to informally assess students after they complete this activity. Students should be able to:

- correctly complete the activity page
- work cooperatively with a partner with changing word spellings
- follow written directions

Change the Words

Directions: Look at the words inside each box. Follow the steps underneath each box to create a new word with those original words.

1. **CAT**

   1. Keep the first letter in the word the same. _____
   2. Change the second letter to the fourth vowel in the alphabet. _____ _____
   3. Change the third letter to the letter that comes before *n* in the alphabet. _____ _____ _____
   4. Add the second letter in the alphabet to the end of the word. _____ _____ _____ _____

   New Word: _____

2. **SAME**

   1. Change the first letter in the word to the letter that comes before it in the alphabet. ___
   2. Switch the first vowel in the word to the fourth vowel in the alphabet. ___ ___
   3. Change the last letter in the word to the letter that comes before *L* in the alphabet.

      _____ _____ _____ _____
   4. Change the third letter in the word to the third letter in the alphabet.

      _____ _____ _____ _____

   New Word: _____

3. **MITTEN**

   1. Change the two double letters in the middle so that they are both the fourth letter of the alphabet. _____ _____ _____ _____ _____ _____
   2. Move the fifth letter in the word to become the sixth letter in the word.

      _____ _____ _____ _____ _____ _____
   3. Change the first letter in the new word to the last letter in the word *cap*.

      _____ _____ _____ _____ _____ _____
   4. Change the first vowel in the word so that it is the same as the vowel in *luck*.

      _____ _____ _____ _____ _____ _____
   5. For the fifth letter in the new word, make it the letter that is in the middle of *old*.

      _____ _____ _____ _____ _____ _____

   New Word: _____

Holiday Story Starters

Activity Length
Approximately 30–45 minutes

Activity Format
Small groups

Standards

Grades K–2 (Writing Standards 1.1–1.6; ELD Standard 2.2)

Grades 3–5 (Writing Standards 1.1–1.6; ELD Standard 2.2)

Language Objective

Students will use English to complete a written story.

Learning Objective

Students will improve their writing skills by creating stories after receiving the beginning of a writing prompt.

Materials

- teacher-prepared holiday story starter
- lined paper, one sheet for each group

Procedure

1. Read to the class a holiday story starter that you have created. For example, "For Valentine's Day, students at Brookside Elementary planned a special celebration. They arrived at school early, even before the teachers…."

2. Divide the class into groups. Have each group work together to complete the story.

3. When groups finish, have students read their stories to the rest of the class. Lead a class discussion of how their stories were similar and different.

Teacher Tips

- Incorporate cultural holidays that reflect the backgrounds of the students in your class.

- Have students create their own story starters for the class to complete. Story starters do not need to be about holidays; they may be about a curriculum theme.

Differentiating by Proficiency Level

Beginning: Give students a simple sentence frame to complete.

Intermediate: Encourage students to add more details to their stories.

Advanced: Have students create their own complex sentences without sentence frames.

To differentiate by proficiency level, see pp. 11–15 for **Bloom's Taxonomy Questions** and pp. 19–24 for detailed examples.

Assessment

The following is a checklist of items to informally assess students after they complete this activity. Students should be able to:

- add detail to their writing
- develop oral presentation skills
- participate in a classroom discussion pertaining to the activity

The Longest Sentence

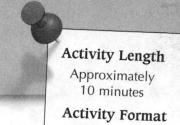

Standards

Grades K–2 (Writing Standards 1.1–1.8; ELD Standard 2.2)

Grades 3–5 (Writing Standards 1.1–1.7; ELD Standard 2.2)

Language Objective

Students will use English to write detailed complete sentences.

Learning Objective

Students will improve editing skills by writing appropriate words in order to complete open-ended sentences.

Materials

- timer
- teacher-prepared sheets of lined paper with the first word of a sentence (e.g., *I*, *My*, *The*, *Once*), one per group

Procedure

1. Divide the class into groups.

2. Give every group a sheet of paper with the same word written on it. For example, the paper might have the word *My*. Set the timer for five minutes. Students should remain silent during this activity. One person in each group takes the paper and writes one word to continue the sentence. That student might write *dog*, so the paper now reads, *My dog*. That student passes the paper to the next student.

3. The next student takes the paper and adds another word, such as *is*, so the paper now reads, *My dog is*. The paper continues until students have completed a sentence. For example, the final sentence might be, *My dog is small and loud*.

4. After all groups are finished, have each group share its sentence. Repeat the process with a new word.

Teacher Tip

- After the timer goes off, ask students to discuss their sentence as a group to see if they agree that it makes sense.

Differentiating by Proficiency Level

Beginning: Give students two choices for responses.

Intermediate: Encourage students to use more descriptive words.

Advanced: Provide complex language structures for students as models.

To differentiate by proficiency level, see pp. 11–15 for **Bloom's Taxonomy Questions** and pp. 19–24 for detailed examples.

Assessment

The following is a checklist of items to informally assess students after they complete this activity. Students should be able to:

- work cooperatively to write detailed complete sentences
- practice critical thinking skills

Object Stories

Activity Length
Approximately 30 minutes

Activity Format
Small groups

Standards

Grades K–2 (Writing Standards 1.1–1.6; ELD Standard 2.2)

Grades 3–5 (Writing Standards 1.1–1.6; ELD Standard 2.2)

Language Objective

Students will use English to write a story that incorporates several random objects.

Learning Objective

Students will develop creative thinking and reasoning skills by creating stories.

Materials

- small random objects brought in by students prior to the activity
- lined paper, one sheet per student

Procedure

1. Divide the class into groups.

2. Have students in each group display their random objects so that the entire group can see.

3. Students each independently write a story that includes all their group's objects. For example, if in a group of four the objects are a *pencil*, a *shoe*, and an *eraser*, the story might start like this: Sandra had an awful problem. While putting on her left *shoe*, she realized that it had various dirt marks on the side. As she looked around the room, she noticed an *eraser*. The thought of erasing the dirt marks crossed her mind...

4. When students finish their stories, they should read them aloud to their group and then discuss how their stories are similar and different.

Teacher Tip

- To introduce a new story, use objects from the story for students to write about.

Differentiating by Proficiency Level

Beginning: Allow students to create simple sentences of their stories. Then help them describe their stories orally.

Intermediate: Have students work in small groups to discuss their stories.

Advanced: Encourage students to use academic language in their written responses.

To differentiate by proficiency level, see pp. 11–15 for **Bloom's Taxonomy Questions** and pp. 19–24 for detailed examples.

Assessment

The following is a checklist of items to informally assess students after they complete this activity. Students should be able to:

- write a story incorporating all of the groups' objects
- practice writing skills by writing a story

So-Close Pictures

Standards

Grades K–2 (Writing Standards 1.1–1.6; ELD Standard 2.2)

Grades 3–5 (Writing Standards 1.1–1.6; ELD Standard 2.2)

Language Objective

Students will use English to write a detailed description about a picture. Students will then read another description and determine which picture matches it.

Learning Objective

Students will develop describing skills as they solve written riddles.

Materials

- copies of page 66, one per student
- lined paper, one sheet per student

Procedure

1. Distribute copies of page 66. Tell students to notice that the pictures are "so-close," yet are different in certain ways.

2. Put students in pairs. Without telling their partner, each student selects one of the six pictures to write a detailed description about. For example, if a student selects the top left-hand picture, he or she might start by writing that the lighthouse is located in the middle. He or she can also write that there is water in the background, and so forth.

3. After each student has written a short description, students will trade papers and try to guess which picture their partner wrote about. If students selected the same picture to write about, have them compare how their descriptions are similar and how they are different.

Teacher Tip

- Have partners work together to draw a new set of So-Close Pictures with new objects in the pictures. Pairs of students may then trade pictures with other students and do the activity as described above.

Differentiating by Proficiency Level

Beginning: Begin by discussing the key vocabulary needed to describe the pictures. Complete the activity orally.

Intermediate: Provide some complex sentence frames to encourage complex responses.

Advanced: Ask students to create their own version of the activity.

To differentiate by proficiency level, see pp. 11–15 for **Bloom's Taxonomy Questions** and pp. 19–24 for detailed examples.

Assessment

The following is a checklist of items to informally assess students after they complete this activity. Students should be able to:

- write a description of the secret picture
- develop understanding of basic positional concepts

Name: _____   Date: _____

So-Close Pictures

Directions: Choose one picture. Write a paragraph describing the picture you selected.

The Fewest Clues

Standards

Grades K–2 (Writing Standard 2.1; ELD Standard 2.1)

Grades 3–5 (Writing Standard 2.1; ELD Standard 2.1)

Language Objective

Students will listen to clues in English about a secret word and then name the secret word.

Learning Objective

Students will increase knowledge about different parts of speech by correctly guessing "secret" words based on clues.

Materials

- copies of page 68, one per student

Procedure

1. Distribute copies of page 68. Tell the class they are going to play a game called "The Fewest Clues." The object of the game is to give different one-word clues about a secret word until students can guess the secret word correctly.

2. Demonstrate an example, such as the one-word clue *barks* for the secret word *dog*. Students should write their guess of what they think the secret word is in the box labeled "Guess #1." The next one-word clue could be *pet*. Students continue to write their guesses. After each clue, they have the opportunity to revise their guess or to leave their answer as is.

3. Continue the process with a new secret word.

Teacher Tips

- To make this game more challenging, you may require that the secret words be a specific part of speech (e.g., adjective, verb, noun).

- Use more complex vocabulary words as you repeat this game throughout the school year.

Differentiating by Proficiency Level

Beginning: Encourage students to draw their responses.

Intermediate: Have students explain their guesses.

Advanced: Ask students to create their own example of the activity for higher-level vocabulary words.

To differentiate by proficiency level, see pp. 11–15 for **Bloom's Taxonomy Questions** and pp. 19–24 for detailed examples.

Assessment

The following is a checklist of items to informally assess students after they complete this activity. Students should be able to:

- guess "secret" words after listening to one-word clues

- practice listening skills as clues are given about a secret word

The Fewest Clues

Directions: Listen carefully to the clues given. Write your guesses for the secret word in the boxes.

ROUND 1	ROUND 2	ROUND 3
Guess #1	**Guess #1**	**Guess #1**
Guess #2	**Guess #2**	**Guess #2**
Guess #3	**Guess #3**	**Guess #3**
Guess #4	**Guess #4**	**Guess #4**
Guess #5	**Guess #5**	**Guess #5**

Idiom Pictures

Standards

Grades K–2 (Writing Standard 8.5; ELD Standard 3.1)

Grades 3–5 (Writing Standard 8.6; ELD Standard 3.1)

Language Objective

Students will use English to discuss idioms and then draw pictures that represent the literal and figurative meaning of their idioms.

Learning Objective

Students will learn the meaning of idioms by comparing the literal and figurative meanings.

Materials

- copies of page 70, one per student
- crayons or markers for each student

Procedure

1. Discuss the meaning of *idiom* (a phrase that has a figurative meaning different from the literal meaning of the individual words in the phrase).

2. Give some examples, such as *tip of the iceberg*, *fork in the road*, *under the weather*, and *face the music*. Discuss both the literal and figurative meanings. Have students help create a list of idioms. Write their responses on the board.

3. Distribute copies of page 70. Have students draw pictures on their paper of idioms with the literal meaning in the left box and the figurative meaning in the right box. Ask students to write at the bottom of their paper what the idiom means. If students cannot think of an idiom to draw, have them select one from the examples.

4. When students have finished, ask them to trade drawings and guess each others' idioms.

Teacher Tip

- Ask students to create new idiom drawings from a list you have provided. Post students' drawings on the wall, for other students to guess.

Differentiating by Proficiency Level

Beginning: Allow students to act out their responses.

Intermediate: Give students multi-step directions to complete the activity.

Advanced: Ask students to draw conclusions about the drawings and idioms.

To differentiate by proficiency level, see pp. 11–15 for **Bloom's Taxonomy Questions** and pp. 19–24 for detailed examples.

Assessment

The following is a checklist of items to informally assess students after they complete this activity. Students should be able to:

- understand figurative language
- practice grammar skills by using idioms correctly
- participate in a classroom discussion pertaining to the definition of *idiom*

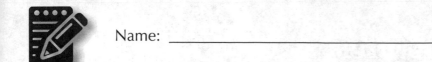

Name: _____ Date: _____

Idiom Pictures

Directions: Draw the picture of the literal meaning of your idiom in the left box. Draw a picture of the figurative meaning in the right box. At the bottom, explain what your idiom means.

Literal Meaning	**Figurative Meaning**

_____

_____

_____

_____

Word Changes

Standards

Grades K–2 (Writing Standards 1.3–1.5; ELD 2.3)

Grades 3–5 (Writing Standards 1.3, 1.4; ELD Standard 2.3)

Language Objective

Students will write English directions to change word spellings and create new words.

Learning Objective

Students will use writing skills to describe how to change one word into another word.

Materials

- teacher-prepared list of 10 words on the board
- copies of page 72, one sheet per student

Procedure

1. Write a list of words on the board. Tell students that they are going to figure out how to change these words into other words.

2. Demonstrate several word changes first. For example, write the word *old* on the board. You might say, "Change the word *old* to a new word by adding the letter *c* to the beginning of it. This makes the word *cold*."

3. Have students work with partners. Distribute copies of page 72. Students should choose a word from the board and decide how to change it. Have them write their instructions on the paper.

4. Once students are done, have them share how they changed each word with the class.

Teacher Tips

- When students change their words, ask them to write a sentence with it.
- Allow students to generate their own list of words and describe how to change them to new words.

Differentiating by Proficiency Level

Beginning: Add labeled pictures to the directions.
Intermediate: Have students discuss each step with a small group.
Advanced: Ask students to create an alternative version of the activity.

To differentiate by proficiency level, see pp. 11–15 for **Bloom's Taxonomy Questions** and pp. 19–24 for detailed examples.

Assessment

The following is a checklist of items to informally assess students after they complete this activity. Students should be able to:

- describe how to change one word into another word
- create written directions

Name: _____ Date: _____

Word Changes

Directions: Select a word your teacher gives you. Write it on the line next to the number. Write at least three steps of how to change your word to a new word. Write the new word on the line.

1. My word _____

　　Step 1: _____

　　Step 2: _____

　　Step 3: _____

　　Step 4: _____

　　New word: _____

2. My word _____

　　Step 1: _____

　　Step 2: _____

　　Step 3: _____

　　Step 4: _____

　　New word: _____

World's Longest Story

Activity Length
Approximately 45 minutes

Activity Format
Whole group

Standards

Grades K–2 (Writing Standards 1.1–1.8; ELD Standard 2.2)

Grades 3–5 (Writing Standards 1.1–1.7; ELD Standard 2.2)

Language Objective

Students will use English to write or dictate sentences that compose a story.

Learning Objective

Students will develop storytelling abilities by working cooperatively to write a story.

Materials

- pictures from magazines already cut out, one picture per student
- chart paper
- tape, a small piece for each student

Procedure

1. Tell students that together they will be making the world's longest story. Distribute pictures to students.

2. Select someone to start the story. Place the first picture on the board. Ask one student to write or dictate a sentence about the picture to start the story. Write that sentence on the chart paper. For example, if the picture is of a family, the story may begin, "One day the Jones family decided to go for a walk."

3. Ask another student to place his or her picture on the board and then write or dictate a second sentence to combine the story. The sentence must make sense in relation to the first sentence.

4. Continue the process and read the ending result.

Teacher Tip

- This activity allows students to use creativity and reasoning skills to help write a story.

Differentiating by Proficiency Level

Beginning: Allow students to discuss in their native languages and then respond in English.

Intermediate: Encourage students to tell more about their pictures.

Advanced: Ask students to respond in writing.

To differentiate by proficiency level, see pp. 11–15 for **Bloom's Taxonomy Questions** and pp. 19–24 for detailed examples.

Assessment

The following is a checklist of items to informally assess students after they complete this activity. Students should be able to:

- participate in a classroom discussion pertaining to the writing activity
- write or dictate sentences
- compose sentences that develop a story

Mathematics

This page is to keep a record of when the activities were taught and what adjustments or modifications were made. This log can be used to keep track of students' progress, to make modifications, and for future planning.

Activities	Notes
ABCs	
Countdown	
Three in a Row	
Daily Math Question	
Math Words	
Let Your Fingers Do the Walking on the Calendar	
Math Circle Memory	
Math High Five	
Math Stand-Up	
Math King/Queen	
Scavenger Hunt	
Time Directions	

ABCs

Activity Length
Approximately 30–45 minutes

Activity Format
Whole group or small groups

Standards

Grades K–2 (Mathematics Standard 2.5; ELD Standard 2.1)

Grades 3–5 (Mathematics Standard 2.2; ELD Standard 2.1)

Language Objective

Students will use English to participate in a classroom discussion about a math topic.

Learning Objective

Students will have a better understanding of the concept of a unit being divided into fractional equal parts.

Materials

- copies of page 76, one per student

Procedure

1. Discuss with students the mathematics topic they are focusing on in class. Have a group discussion of what they know about the topic and what they would like to know.

2. Distribute copies of page 76. Have students write the mathematics topic in the center box. For example, if they are learning about fractions, they would write *fraction* in the Mathematics Topic box, and fill in the chart according to the mathematics topic. The word *pizza* could be placed under *P*, *divide* could go under *D*, and so on.

3. Discuss the answers that students wrote in their charts.

Teacher Tips

- The first time this activity is done, provide students with a word or two as examples before they participate.

- This activity can be used as a word wall. Enlarge the activity sheet so it can be placed in the classroom to help students have a better understanding of the new topic.

Differentiating by Proficiency Level

Beginning: Use the whole-group format to allow students to hear the discussion.

Intermediate: Ask students to say some words related to the topic.

Advanced: Ask students to defend and support their choices.

To differentiate by proficiency level, see pp. 11–15 for **Bloom's Taxonomy Questions** and pp. 19–24 for detailed examples.

Assessment

The following is a checklist of items to informally assess students after they complete this activity. Students should be able to:

- have a better understanding of the mathematics theme

- participate in a classroom discussion pertaining to the mathematics topic

Name: _____ Date: _____

ABCs

Directions: Think about the mathematics topic. Write the mathematics topic in the center box. Fill in the other boxes with words that start with the letter shown in each box.

A	B	C
D	**E**	**F**
G	**Mathematics Topic**	**H**
I		**J**
K		**L**
M		**N**
O	**P**	**Q**
R	**S**	**T**
U	**V**	**W**
X	**Y**	**Z**

#50203—Activities for English Language Learners Across the Curriculum   © *Shell Education*

Countdown

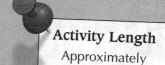

Activity Length
Approximately
10 minutes

Activity Format
Whole group or
small groups

Standards

Grades K–2 (Mathematics
Standard 2.2;
ELD Standard 2.1)

Grades 3–5 (Mathematics
Standard 9.1;
ELD Standard 2.1)

Language Objective

Students will use English
to listen to and follow
directions.

Learning Objective

Students will be able to
use auditory memory
skills to understand
that numbers and the
operations performed
on them can be used to
describe things in the real
world.

Materials

- none

Procedure

1. Demonstrate to students what a "countdown" is (e.g., 10, 9, 8, 7, 6, and so on).

2. Give students a simple direction such as, "When I count down to seven, clap your hands." Begin counting down, and when you get to seven, students should clap their hands.

3. Continue with as many directions as you would like, varying the starting and ending numbers each time.

Teacher Tips

- Prior to the activity, create a "cheat sheet" on which the directions are already written for students who may need it, or write the directions on the board.

- Modify this activity by shortening the directions so that students who may not understand can still participate and remember them.

Differentiating by Proficiency Level

Beginning: Model each direction first (such as clapping your hands).

Intermediate: Give students multi-step directions to complete the activity.

Advanced: Ask students to create their own directions.

To differentiate by proficiency level, see pp. 11–15 for **Bloom's Taxonomy Questions** and pp. 19–24 for detailed examples.

Assessment

The following is a checklist of items to informally assess students after they complete this activity. Students should be able to:

- follow oral directions

- correctly identify numbers as they hear them

- practice auditory memory skills by following directions

Three in a Row

Activity Length
Approximately 45 minutes

Activity Format
Whole group

Standards

Grades K–2 (Mathematics Standards 1.4; ELD Standard 2.2)

Grades 3–5 (Mathematics Standards 1.3; ELD Standard 2.2)

Language Objective

Students will use English to practice vocabulary by writing words and listening for clues about them.

Learning Objective

Students will reinforce their knowledge of newly acquired vocabulary by participating in a traditional game and use the vocabulary terms to improve their writing skills.

Materials

- vocabulary words from the current mathematics unit posted on a chart or on the board
- teacher-prepared sentences — one sentence that shows the meaning of each vocabulary word without using the word
- copies of page 79, one per student

Procedure

1. Distribute copies of page 79. Have students write in the squares different vocabulary words from the current mathematics unit.

2. Read a sentence to students and ask them to put an *X* in the square for the word that matches the sentence. For example, if a student wrote the vocabulary word *right angle* in a square and the sentence read aloud was, "The class knew what kind of angle it was because it was 90 degrees," the student would draw an *X* in that square. When a student gets three *X*s in a row (horizontally, vertically, or diagonally), he or she calls out, "Three in a row!" and the game is over.

Teacher Tips

- As an extended activity, have students create sentences with the vocabulary words.
- Have students draw a picture of the word to help with comprehension.

Differentiating by Proficiency Level

Beginning: Use shorter sentences for the activity.

Intermediate: Have students work in groups or with a partner to find the words.

Advanced: Ask students to explain how their knowledge about the topic has changed.

To differentiate by proficiency level, see pp. 11–15 for **Bloom's Taxonomy Questions** and pp. 19–24 for detailed examples.

Assessment

The following is a checklist of items to informally assess students after they complete this activity. Students should be able to:

- write selected vocabulary words
- recognize correct usage of mathematical vocabulary terms

Name: _____ Date: _____

Three in a Row

Directions: Fill in the boxes with words given by your teacher. Listen to each sentence. If the sentence tells about a word in a box, put an *X* in the box. When you get three *X*s in a row (horizontally, vertically, diagonally), call out, "Three in a row!"

Daily Math Question

Standards

Grades K–2 (Mathematics Standard 1.2; ELD Standard 2.1)

Grades 3–5 (Mathematics Standards 1.3, 1.4, 1.7; ELD Standard 2.1)

Language Objective

Students will use English to listen to and respond to questions about a math topic.

Learning Objective

Students will be able to develop reasoning and creative thinking skills by generating math questions for the class to solve.

Materials

- teacher-prepared daily math question

Procedure

1. Ask a daily math question at the beginning of the math lesson (already created prior to math instructional time). Write this question on the board. Questions should pertain to the topic students are currently studying. For example, if students are currently studying measurement, a question you may ask is, "How many ounces are in four pounds?"

2. Students will use reasoning skills to answer the question. With the example question above, students can use their math textbooks or notes they may have as a reference. Once they realize that there are 16 ounces in one pound, they can use reasoning skills to solve the problem. Encourage students to check their reasoning and answers with classmates.

3. At the end of the math lesson, have students share their answers to the question and discuss how they found their answers.

Teacher Tip

- Each day after you have given the daily math question, give one student a chance to create a daily math question for the rest of the class to solve the next day.

Differentiating by Proficiency Level

Beginning: Allow students to draw their responses.

Intermediate: Encourage students to answer in complete sentences.

Advanced: Ask students to defend and support their choices.

To differentiate by proficiency level, see pp. 11–15 for **Bloom's Taxonomy Questions** and pp. 19–24 for detailed examples.

Assessment

The following is a checklist of items to informally assess students after they complete this activity. Students should be able to:

- develop reasoning and creative skills by responding to questions about a math topic

- participate in classroom discussion pertaining to the activity

- explain to others how the problem was solved

Math Words

Standards

Grades K–2 (Mathematics Standards 1.4, 2.4; ELD Standard 2.1)

Grades 3–5 (Mathematics Standard 1.2; ELD Standard 2.1)

Language Objective

Students will use English to listen to and follow directions to spell math words.

Learning Objective

Students will be able to follow directions with ordinal numbers and determine an unknown word or sentence.

Materials

- copies of page 82, one per student
- teacher-prepared list of mathematics vocabulary words
- alphabet chart or poster for students' reference

Procedure

1. Review ordinal numbers with students at the beginning of the lesson. Ask questions such as, "What is the fourth letter of the alphabet? (D) The sixth? (E) The ninth? (I)"

2. Distribute copies of page 82.

3. Choose a mathematics vocabulary word from your list. Don't tell students the word. Starting with the first round, give directions about what letters to put in the boxes using ordinal numbers. For example, for the word *decimal*, say, "First write the fourth letter of the alphabet. Next, write the fifth letter. Then write the third letter." Continue until the word is spelled.

Teacher Tip

- This is a great activity to use to introduce vocabulary words.

Differentiating by Proficiency Level

Beginning: Preview ordinal numbers with students before beginning the activity. Give students an alphabet chart.

Intermediate: Encourage students to work in groups. They should discuss the answer to each step.

Advanced: Ask students to summarize their learning with complete sentences.

To differentiate by proficiency level, see pp. 11–15 for **Bloom's Taxonomy Questions** and pp. 19–24 for detailed examples.

Assessment

The following is a checklist of items to informally assess students after they complete this activity. Students should be able to:

- develop an understanding of ordinal numbers
- practice listening skills by following directions to spell mathematical words
- follow oral directions

Math Words

Directions: Listen carefully to your teacher's directions. Fill in the boxes with letters to spell out mathematics vocabulary words as the directions are given to you.

ROUND 1

ROUND 2

ROUND 3

ROUND 4

Let Your Fingers Do the Walking on the Calendar

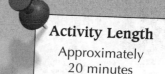

Activity Length
Approximately
20 minutes

Activity Format
Whole group, then
partners

Standards

Grades K–2 (Mathematics
Standard 6.1, 6.2;
ELD Standard 2.2)

Grades 3–5 (Mathematics
Standard 6.1;
ELD Standard 2.2)

Language Objective

Students will use English
to listen to and follow
directions to build their
knowledge about a
calendar.

Learning Objective

Students will have a
better understanding of
the concept of a calendar
by accurately giving and
receiving oral directions.

Materials

- copies of page 84, one per student (You may choose to modify this page from the Teacher Resource CD.)

Procedure

1. Distribute copies of page 84. Tell students that they will do an activity where they let their fingers do the walking on the calendar. Take a moment to discuss what this means.

2. Give students directions to follow such as, "Place your finger on the second Tuesday of the month, and then move it backward one week." Each student's finger should be placed on the correct answer. Continue with more directions.

3. After you feel students are comfortable with the activity, place them in pairs.

4. Partners take turns giving each other a series of calendar directions. Have students check to see if their partner is correct.

Teacher Tips

- Use this activity to review key concepts of a calendar with the class.

- You can use the calendar to relate it to events that are taking place at school.

Differentiating by Proficiency Level

Beginning: Ask students to circle the correct answer at each step.

Intermediate: Encourage students to give their calendar directions.

Advanced: Ask students to paraphrase another student's response.

To differentiate by proficiency level, see pp. 11–15 for **Bloom's Taxonomy Questions** and pp. 19–24 for detailed examples.

Assessment

The following is a checklist of items to informally assess students after they complete this activity. Students should be able to:

- listen to and follow oral directions

- demonstrate an understanding of a calendar by correctly answering questions

Name: _____   Date: _____

Let Your Fingers Do the Walking on the Calendar

Directions: Listen carefully to your partner for directions. Use your calendar as a guide to find the correct answers.

Su	M	T	W	Th	F	Sa
				1	2	3
4	5	6	7	8	9	10
11	12	13	14	15	16	17
18	19	20	21	22	23	24
25	26	27	28	29	30	31

Math Circle Memory

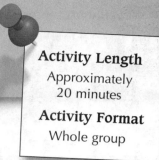

Standards

Grades K–2 (Mathematics Standard 2.4; ELD Standard 2.2)

Grades 3–5 (Mathematics Standard 1.2; ELD Standard 2.2)

Language Objective

Students will listen to directions in English and follow them.

Learning Objective

Students will be able to develop auditory memory skills and correctly follow oral directions.

Materials

* scratch paper, one sheet per student

Procedure

1. Seat the students in a circle with pencils and scratch paper.

2. Tell students to listen carefully to your directions and to follow them exactly.

3. Give a direction using math such as, "When I touch Lucas on the shoulder, everyone should count backward from 12 to 4." Walk around the circle and touch one student on the shoulder. Students must remember your direction and demonstrate it.

4. Continue with another math direction such as, "When I touch Cindy on the shoulder, everyone will solve this problem: 8 + 6." Continue with more directions.

Teacher Tip

* To extend the activity, allow students to create some examples of their own to share with the class.

Differentiating by Proficiency Level

Beginning: Show students the math equation in writing as you say it.

Intermediate: Have students write their answers and read them aloud.

Advanced: Ask students to create their own examples of the activity.

To differentiate by proficiency level, see pp. 11–15 for **Bloom's Taxonomy Questions** and pp. 19–24 for detailed examples.

Assessment

The following is a checklist of items to informally assess students after they complete this activity. Students should be able to:

* develop auditory memory skills by correctly completing multi-step directions

* follow oral directions

* practice listening skills by following oral directions

Math High Five

Activity Length
Approximately 10 minutes

Activity Format
Whole group, small groups, partners, or independent

Standards

Grades K–2 (Mathematics Standards 1.1–1.4; ELD Standard 2.2)

Grades 3–5 (Mathematics Standards 1.1–1.4; ELD Standard 2.2)

Language Objective

Students will use English to solve problems with a five-step process.

Learning Objective

Students will have a better understanding of how to solve mathematical equations with the help of a guide.

Materials

- copies of page 87, one per student
- teacher-prepared mathematical word problem
- scissors

Procedure

1. Distribute copies of page 87.

2. Select a mathematical word problem you would like students to solve. Write the word problem on the board. For example, "Jack had 13 marbles, but gave four to Lou and three to Steve, how many marbles does he have left?"

3. Have students cut out their math hand and use it as a guide to solve the word problem. Starting with the pinky and working from left to right, model for students how to properly use the activity page. The first step asks you to repeat what you have to find. For the example problem written above, students would state that they have to find out how many marbles Jack has in all. Step two asks students to find the facts. For this example, the facts are that Jack had 13 marbles, but then he gave four to Lou and three to Steve. Step three asks students to select a strategy. Continue with the remaining steps.

4. Discuss with students the answer and the steps.

Teacher Tip

- The first few times, model for students how to correctly use this strategy.

Differentiating by Proficiency Level

Beginning: Repeat key vocabulary words in a systematic way.

Intermediate: Encourage students to answer in complete sentences.

Advanced: Ask students to defend and support their answers.

To differentiate by proficiency level, see pp. 11–15 for **Bloom's Taxonomy Questions** and pp. 19–24 for detailed examples.

Assessment

The following is a checklist of items to informally assess students after they complete this activity. Students should be able to:

- correctly solve mathematical word problems
- demonstrate problem-solving strategies by following the five-step process

Math High Five

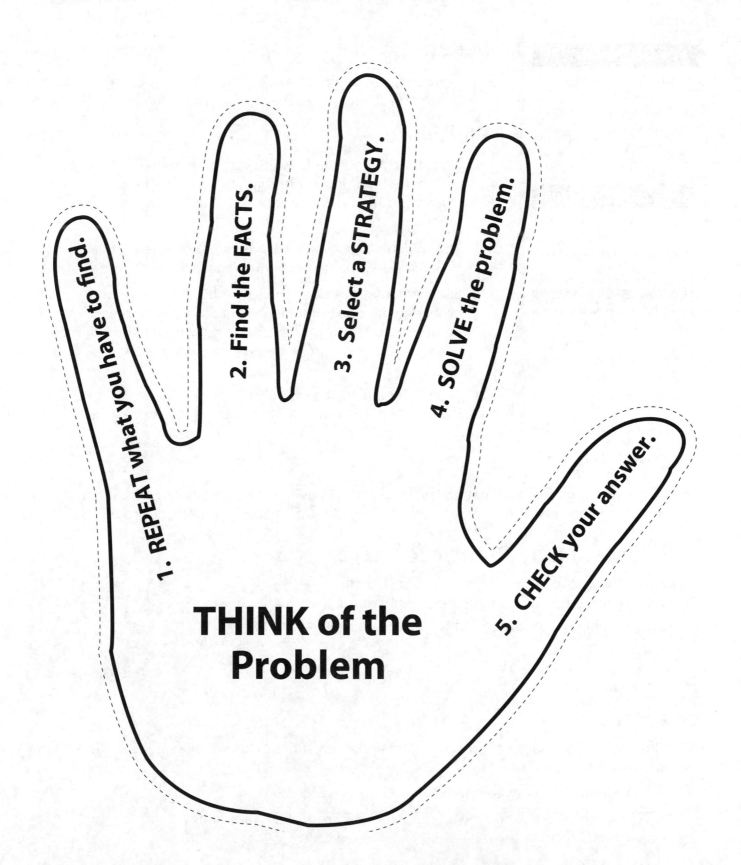

1. REPEAT what you have to find.

2. Find the FACTS.

3. Select a STRATEGY.

4. SOLVE the problem.

5. CHECK your answer.

THINK of the Problem

Math Stand-Up

Activity Length
Approximately
10 minutes

Activity Format
Whole group or
small groups

Standards

Grades K–2 (Mathematics
Standards 1.2, 1.3;
ELD Standard 2.2)

Grades 3–5 (Mathematics
Standards 1.1, 1.2;
ELD Standard 2.2)

Language Objective

Students will listen for
their names and use
English to connect and
explain information.

Learning Objective

Students will be able to
develop categorization
skills by orally describing
a reason why a group
of numbers or math
problems are similar.

Materials

- numbers or math problems (e.g., 6 + 3 =___, 8 – 4 =___)
  written on sheets of papers, one per student

Procedure

1. Seat students in a circle with each student holding a sheet
   of paper with a number or math problem written on it. Ask
   students to hold up their papers so that everyone can see
   them.

2. Tell students that you will say the names of selected students.
   If you say their name, they must stand up.

3. Say the names of students who are holding a number or math
   problem with one common attribute. For example, say the
   names of students who have numbers with a two in the tens
   place or who have problems with the same answer
   (e.g., 10 - 5 = ___, 3 + 2 = ___).

4. Everyone must look at the papers of students standing and
   determine what is similar about the numbers or problems.

Teacher Tip

- Do not mix numbers and math problems for this activity; either all students should hold a
  paper with a number on it, or all students should hold a paper with a math problem on it.

Differentiating by Proficiency Level

Beginning: Allow students to point to and/or draw the
similarities among the selected numbers or problems.

Intermediate: Encourage students to tell more about their
answers.

Advanced: Ask students to use complex language structures
in their comparisons.

To differentiate by proficiency
level, see pp. 11–15 for
Bloom's Taxonomy Questions
and pp. 19–24 for detailed
examples.

Assessment

The following is a checklist of items to informally assess students after they complete this activity.
Students should be able to:

- identify similarities between numbers and math problems

- orally describe the reason why a group of numbers or math problems are similar

Math King/Queen

Standards

Grades K–2 (Mathematics Standard 1.2; ELD Standard 2.2)

Grades 3–5 (Mathematics Standard 1.1; ELD Standard 2.2)

Language Objective

Students will use English to listen to and follow multi-step directions.

Learning Objective

Students will be able to follow multi-step directions and correctly solve math problems.

Materials

- crown made from page 90

Procedure

1. Prior to the activity, on a piece of sturdy paper, create a crown by tracing the crown cut out on page 90.

2. Give a series of directions related to math (e.g., *write an odd number on the board, count by fives until you get to 25, write a number larger than 1,000 on the board*). The directions do not have to relate to each other.

3. Select one student to follow the directions. If that student follows your series of math directions correctly, then he or she wears the crown. That student continues wearing the crown until another student correctly follows a new series of math directions. The student then passes on the crown, or if you like, give another crown for that student to wear.

Teacher Tip

- Start with simple directions and progress with directions that have multiple steps. Be sure to target math skills that you have been learning.

Differentiating by Proficiency Level

Beginning: State the direction in short, simple sentences with familiar vocabulary.

Intermediate: Have students explain their answers.

Advanced: State directions in compound or complex sentences with more challenging vocabulary.

To differentiate by proficiency level, see pp. 11–15 for **Bloom's Taxonomy Questions** and pp. 19–24 for detailed examples.

Assessment

The following is a checklist of items to informally assess students after they complete this activity. Students should be able to:

- practice following multi-step directions

- practice listening skills by following oral directions

- practice auditory memory skills by completing multi-step directions

Math King/Queen

Scavenger Hunt

Standards

Grades K–2 (Mathematics Standards 1.2, 2.1; ELD Standard 2.2)

Grades 3–5 (Mathematics Standards 1.1, 1.3, 6.1; ELD Standard 2.2)

Language Objective

Students will work together to find items. They will use English to discuss the topic.

Learning Objective

Students will develop categorization and vocabulary skills by working cooperatively and communicating effectively in small groups while completing a scavenger hunt pertaining to a current math topic.

Materials

- copies of a teacher-prepared scavenger hunt list created prior to activity, related to a current unit of study in mathematics, one per group

Procedure

1. Discuss with the class what a scavenger hunt is (a game in which people must find a variety of items on a list). Tell students they will be working in groups to find a list of math items.

2. Divide the class into groups. Give each group a copy of the scavenger hunt list you have created. Students will work together to find as many items as possible from the list. For example, for measurement, create a list specifically telling students what they should find (something that is 2 inches long, 6 inches long, etc.).

3. After a set amount of time, have groups answer questions about the scavenger hunt such as, "Which item(s) was easiest/ hardest to find? Why?" Discuss how the items connect to an area of study.

Teacher Tips

- Have students create their own scavenger lists pertaining to a math topic.

- As students are working, make sure you monitor and help groups who are having difficulty finding the items on the list.

Differentiating by Proficiency Level

Beginning: Preview the list with students in a small group.

Intermediate: During the discussion at the end of the activity ask students to say other words related to the topic.

Advanced: Ask students to defend and support their choices.

To differentiate by proficiency level, see pp. 11–15 for **Bloom's Taxonomy Questions** and pp. 19–24 for detailed examples.

Assessment

The following is a checklist of items to informally assess students after they complete this activity. Students should be able to:

- work cooperatively to find items related to a current unit of study

- participate in a classroom discussion pertaining to the unit of study

Time Directions

Standards

Grades K–2 (Mathematics Standards 4.2, 4.3; ELD Standard 2.2)

Grades 3–5 (Mathematics Standards 1.1, 1.3; ELD Standard 2.2)

Language Objective

Students will use English to listen to and give and follow directions.

Learning Objective

Students will reinforce the concept of telling time by correctly giving and following oral directions.

Materials

- copy of page 93
- crayons or markers for each student

Procedure

1. Distribute copies of page 93. Tell students to listen carefully and to follow your directions on how to complete the activity.

2. Give students one set of oral directions such as, "It is 1:30. A half hour passes. Color the clock red that shows what time it is now."

3. Have students work with partners, taking turns giving and following oral directions with each other to complete the page.

Teacher Tips

- Review vocabulary terms related to time.
- Model the activity with a clock as a visual.

Differentiating by Proficiency Level

Beginning: Ask students to first point to the correct answer. Check their answers.

Intermediate: Ask students to label their clocks.

Advanced: Ask students to defend and support their answers.

To differentiate by proficiency level, see pp. 11–15 for **Bloom's Taxonomy Questions** and pp. 19–24 for detailed examples.

Assessment

The following is a checklist of items to informally assess students after they complete this activity. Students should be able to:

- follow oral directions
- practice listening skills by following oral directions
- reinforce the concept of telling time by correctly giving directions

Name: _____ Date: _____

Time Directions

Directions: Listen carefully to the directions. Color the clocks to show the correct answers.

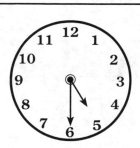

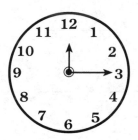
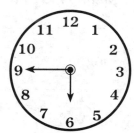

Science

This page is to keep a record of when the activities were taught and what adjustments or modifications were made. This log can be used to keep track of students' progress, to make modifications, and for future planning.

Activities	Notes
ABCs	
Auditory Memory Game	
Bingo	
Science Maze	
Science Similes	
Science Swap	
Science Synonyms	
Science Vocabulary	
Secret Science Box	
Textures	
Three in a Row	
True/False Science	

ABCs

Standards

Grades K–2 (Science Standards 1.0, 13.1; ELD Standard 2.2)

Grades 3–5 (Science Standards 1.0, 3.0, 12.2; ELD Standard 2.2)

Language Objective

Students will use English to participate in a classroom discussion about a science theme.

Learning Objective

Students will have a better understanding of some vocabulary words pertaining to the water cycle

Materials

- copies of page 96, one per student

Procedure

1. Discuss with students the science theme they will be learning. Have a group discussion of what they know about the topic and what they would like to know.

2. Distribute copies of page 96. Have students write the science topic in the center box. For example, with the water cycle theme, students would write *water cycle* in the Science Topic box and fill in the chart according to the topic. They could place the word *rain* under *R*, *evaporation* under *E*, and so on.

3. Discuss the answers that students placed in their charts.

Teacher Tips

- The first time this activity is done, provide students with a word or two as examples before they participate.

- This activity can be used as a word wall. Enlarge the activity sheet so it can be placed in the classroom to help students have a better understanding of the new topic.

Differentiating by Proficiency Level

Beginning: Use the whole-group format to allow students to hear the discussion.

Intermediate: Ask students to say some words related to the topic.

Advanced: Ask students to defend and support their choices.

To differentiate by proficiency level, see pp. 11–15 for **Bloom's Taxonomy Questions** and pp. 19–24 for detailed examples.

Assessment

The following is a checklist of items to informally assess students after they complete this activity. Students should be able to:

- have a better understanding of the science theme

- participate in a classroom discussion pertaining to the science theme

Name: _____   Date: _____

ABCs

Directions: Think about the science topic. Write the science topic in the center box. Fill in the other boxes with words that start with the letter shown in each box.

A	B	C
D	**E**	**F**
G	**Science Topic**	**H**
I		**J**
K		**L**
M		**N**
O	**P**	**Q**
R	**S**	**T**
U	**V**	**W**
X	**Y**	**Z**

Auditory Memory Game

Activity Length
Approximately 20 minutes

Activity Format
Whole group

Standards

Grades K–2 (Science Standards 3.0, 13.1; ELD Standard 2.1)

Grades 3–5 (Science Standards 3.0, 12.1; ELD Standard 2.1)

Language Objective

Students will use English to interact in the classroom by listening and participating in group discussions.

Learning Objective

Students will be able to learn fun facts by developing categorization skills regarding an area of study.

Materials

- none

Procedure

1. Tell students they are going to play a memory game.

2. Select a starter phrase for this game that is related to your current science topic. For example, for an ocean unit the starter phrase might be, "On a trip to the ocean, I saw...."

3. Select one student to say the starter phrase and name an appropriate science word to complete the phrase. For example, "On a trip to the ocean, I saw a dolphin." The next student repeats what the first student said and adds a word to the list. "On a trip to the ocean, I saw a dolphin and a tidal wave."

4. Continue the process until all students have had a turn.

Teacher Tips

- Have pictures or models of the objects as visuals to help students.

- Write science vocabulary words on the board for reference.

Differentiating by Proficiency Level

Beginning: Add labeled pictures as visuals.

Intermediate: Provide more complex sentence frames to encourage complex responses.

Advanced: Ask students to paraphrase another student's response.

To differentiate by proficiency level, see pp. 11–15 for **Bloom's Taxonomy Questions** and pp. 19–24 for detailed examples.

Assessment

The following is a checklist of items to informally assess students after they complete this activity. Students should be able to:

- practice auditory memory skills by stating phrases stated by classmates

- participate in a classroom discussion pertaining to the science theme

- state a fact they learned regarding the area of study

Bingo

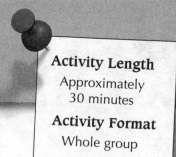

Standards

Grades K–2 (Science Standards 4.1, 4.2, 5.0, 13.1; ELD Standard 2.2)

Grades 3–5 (Science Standards 4.1, 5.0, 12.2; ELD Standard 2.2)

Language Objective

Students will use English to practice vocabulary by writing words and listening for clues about them.

Learning Objective

Students will be able to check their knowledge on a particular subject by playing a traditional game.

Materials

- copies of page 99, one per student

Procedure

1. Distribute copies of page 99. Have students complete the chart with vocabulary terms based on a particular topic in science. For example, if you were teaching the theme of plants, students would fill out the chart with vocabulary terms such as, *seed, leaf, roots, photosynthesis, sunlight,* etc.

2. Read the definition of one vocabulary word. If the definition matches a word in the box, have students place an *X* in that box. For example, with the vocabulary word *seed,* the definition might be, "The source of development or growth."

3. Once a student has a Bingo (five *X*s diagonally, horizontally, or vertically), have him or her say, "Bingo!"

Teacher Tip

- This is a great activity to do before introducing a theme as a pre-assessment. This will allow you to have a better understanding of what students already know about a particular subject.

Differentiating by Proficiency Level

Beginning: Show pictures as you state each definition to improve comprehension.

Intermediate: Ask students to say some words related to the topic.

Advanced: Ask students to defend and support their choices.

To differentiate by proficiency level, see pp. 11–15 for **Bloom's Taxonomy Questions** and pp. 19–24 for detailed examples.

Assessment

The following is a checklist of items to informally assess students after they complete this activity. Students should be able to:

- demonstrate prior knowledge on a particular subject by participating in the game
- practice listening skills by writing words and listening for clues about them

Bingo

Directions: Fill in the boxes with words given by your teacher. Listen to the sentence. If the definition matches a word in a box, put an X in the box. When you get bingo (five Xs diagonally, horizontally, or vertically) say, "Bingo!"

B	I	N	G	O

Science Maze

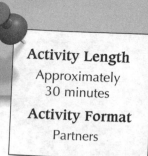

Standards

Grades K–2 (Science
Standard 5.2;
ELD Standard 2.2)

Grades 3–5 (Science
Standard 5.2;
ELD Standard 2.2)

Language Objective

Students will use English
to give and follow oral
directions.

Learning Objective

Students will be able
to state why some
objects and animals are
dangerous to touch.

Materials

• copies of page 101, one per student

Procedure

1. Distribute copies of page 101. Discuss with students why they would not want to touch each animal or object shown in the maze. Explain how the animals might protect themselves if they were touched.

2. Tell students their job is to move their fingers through the maze and make it safely from start to finish without touching one of the animals or dangerous objects. However, students will have to do so with their eyes closed. The only way they will be able to successfully complete the maze is to listen to their partner's directions on where to move their fingers.

3. Divide the class into pairs. One student in each pair must give directions while the other student follows the directions with their eyes closed. Students trade roles after successfully completing the maze.

Teacher Tip

• Give students a chance to create their own science mazes with science-related objects beside the path. Encourage students to research different objects for this activity.

Differentiating by Proficiency Level

Beginning: Allow students to first discuss in their native languages and then respond in English.

Intermediate: Encourage students to answer in complete sentences.

Advanced: Ask students to paraphrase what they have learned.

To differentiate by proficiency level, see pp. 11–15 for **Bloom's Taxonomy Questions** and pp. 19–24 for detailed examples.

Assessment

The following is a checklist of items to informally assess students after they complete this activity. Students should be able to:

• follow oral directions

• state how animals physically protect themselves

• state why some objects are dangerous to touch

Science Maze

Directions: Listen carefully to your partner to know exactly where to move your finger on the maze.

Science Similes

Standards

Grades K–2 (Science Standards 7.1, 13.1; ELD Standard 2.2)

Grades 3–5 (Science Standards 7.1, 11.2; ELD Standard 2.2)

Language Objective

Students will use English to describe objects using similes.

Learning Objective

Students will have a better understanding of dinosaurs by using and sharing background knowledge to create similes.

Materials

- a list of nouns related to a science theme
- scratch paper, one sheet per pair of students

Procedure

1. Discuss the meaning of a simile with the class (comparing two things using the phrase "as ___ as ___"). Share examples such as, "Her hair was as brown as chocolate." Have students help create more examples of similes. Write their responses on the board.

2. Have students work in pairs to generate some similes about nouns from your current science theme. Tell students to keep their similes a secret from the rest of the class until it is time to share. A good tip to tell students is to start with, "I am thinking of..."

3. When sharing, students must not name the answer as part of their simile. For example, a student might say, "I'm thinking of a dinosaur that has a plate as sharp as pointed metal. What dinosaur am I thinking of?" (Answer: Stegosaurus). Other students try to guess which science noun was described by each simile.

Teacher Tip

- Repeat this activity throughout the year as the class studies different science themes.

Differentiating by Proficiency Level

Beginning: Provide choices for completing similes.
Intermediate: Have students explain their similes.
Advanced: Ask students to draw conclusions about the topic.

To differentiate by proficiency level, see pp. 11–15 for **Bloom's Taxonomy Questions** and pp. 19–24 for detailed examples.

Assessment

The following is a checklist of items to informally assess students after they complete this activity. Students should be able to:

- practice describing skills by using similes to describe objects
- develop grammar skills by creating similes using the form "as ___ as ___."

Science Swap

Activity Length
Approximately 25–30 minutes

Activity Format
Whole group

Standards

Grades K–2 (Science Standards 7.1, 13.1; ELD Standard 2.1)

Grades 3–5 (Science Standards 7.1, 11.2; ELD Standard 2.1)

Language Objective

Students will use English to follow directions and then describe what is seen in pictures.

Learning Objective

Students will reinforce science vocabulary and knowledge, improve ability to follow oral directions, and improve the ability to give accurate oral directions.

Materials

- pictures related to current science topic (one picture per student)

Procedure

1. Place students in a circle. Distribute pictures related to the current science topic.

2. Tell students that they will be swapping their pictures with other students, but they must listen carefully to the directions.

3. Give swapping directions. For example, with an animal theme, you might say, "Students holding a picture of a warm-blooded animal trade with someone who is holding a picture of a cold-blooded animal."

4. After pictures have been swapped, have students describe the new picture they have, including facts or information that they have learned during the science unit.

5. Repeat the process with a new swapping direction.

Teacher Tip

- Repeat this activity with different science themes throughout the school year.

Differentiating by Proficiency Level

Beginning: Label the pictures for the activity. Review some key attributes that will be needed to follow the directions.

Intermediate: Have students work as a group to categorize their pictures.

Advanced: Provide complex language structures for students as models.

To differentiate by proficiency level, see pp. 11–15 for **Bloom's Taxonomy Questions** and pp. 19–24 for detailed examples.

Assessment

The following is a checklist of items to informally assess students after they complete this activity. Students should be able to:

- follow oral directions by correctly trading pictures with classmates

- participate in a classroom discussion pertaining to the science unit

Science Synonyms

Activity Length
Approximately 30–45 minutes

Activity Format
Whole group, then small groups

Standards

Grades K–2 (Science Standards 7.2, 13.1 ELD Standard 2.2)

Grades 3–5 (Science Standards 7.2, 11.2 –ELD Standard 2.2)

Language Objective

Students will use English to think of and write synonyms. Students will also categorize words.

Learning Objective

Students will have a better understanding of various ways to group living things while reinforcing the concept of synonyms.

Materials

- copies of page 105, one per group

Procedure

1. Copy the table from page 105 on the board. Tell students that they will be thinking of science synonyms. For examples, if you are studying forces and motion, select the word *move* as the key word. What words tell how people *move*? (*walk, tiptoe, march, skip,* etc.) What words tell how birds *move*? (*fly, soar, flap, glide,* etc.) Write these words in each quadrant.

2. Divide the class into groups. Distribute one copy of page 105 to each group. Based on your current science unit, provide the key word students are to use. Have groups write the key word at the top of their paper. As a class, discuss which four categories to use for that key word. Each group should write categories at the top of each box. Students in each group should work together to complete the chart, filling in as many synonyms as possible for the key word you selected under each of the categories.

3. After groups complete their charts, have students take turns reading a list of words under one of their categories.

Teacher Tip

- Allow time for discussion to extend the lesson from words to complete sentences.

Differentiating by Proficiency Level

Beginning: Allow students to draw or act out their responses before they are added to their group chart.

Intermediate: Encourage students to use their synonyms in complete sentences.

Advanced: Ask students to paraphrase what they have learned.

To differentiate by proficiency level, see pp. 11–15 for **Bloom's Taxonomy Questions** and pp. 19–24 for detailed examples.

Assessment

The following is a checklist of items to informally assess students after they complete this activity. Students should be able to:

- understands the definition of the word *synonym* to generate a list of synonyms

- categorize words by topic

Name: _____   Date: _____

Science Synonyms

Directions: Write the key word. Then write the four categories. Fill in the chart with as many synonyms as possible for the key word under each of the categories.

Key Word: _____

_____	_____
_____	_____
_____	_____
_____	_____
_____	_____
_____	_____
_____	_____
_____	_____
_____	_____
_____	_____
_____	_____

Science Vocabulary

Activity Length
Approximately
45 minutes

Activity Format
Whole group or
small groups

Standards

Grades K–2 (Science Standards 7.1, 13.1; ELD Standard 2.2)

Grades 3–5 (Science Standards 7.1, 11.2; ELD Standard 2.2)

Language Objective

Students will use English to find out new information using research and discuss their findings.

Learning Objective

Students will learn new vocabulary words and work cooperatively with fellow classmates while doing simple research.

Materials

- display of science objects or pictures for a science theme
- scissors for each student
- copies of page 107, one per student

Procedure

1. For a new science unit, display a group of objects or pictures about that theme for students to see.

2. Distribute copies of page 107. Have students write their name on the lines in each box, and have students cut out their question mark boxes. Tell them to place a question mark paper in front of any objects or pictures they do not recognize.

3. Rather than simply telling students the names of unknown objects, tell students it is their job to do simple research in their textbooks to determine the names of the items they do not know.

4. After the research, discuss with students their findings.

Teacher Tip

- An alternative to this activity is to use sticky notes.

Differentiating by Proficiency Level

Beginning: Ask students to research the names of objects that can be easily found via photos, graphics, etc.

Intermediate: Have students draw a picture and label it to explain their research.

Advanced: Ask students to explain how they did their research.

To differentiate by proficiency level, see pp. 11–15 for **Bloom's Taxonomy Questions** and pp. 19–24 for detailed examples.

Assessment

The following is a checklist of items to informally assess students after they complete this activity. Students should be able to:

- state scientific knowledge they have acquired
- complete simple research skills

Science Vocabulary

Directions: Write your name on the lines in each box. Cut out the boxes below. Place a question mark in front of something you do not recognize.

?	?	?
_____	_____	_____
?	?	?
_____	_____	_____
?	?	?
_____	_____	_____
?	?	?
_____	_____	_____
?	?	?
_____	_____	_____

Secret Science Box

Standards

Grades K–2 (Science Standard 13.1; ELD Standard 2.2)

Grades 3–5 (Science Standard 11.2; ELD Standard 2.2)

Language Objective

Students will use English to ask questions about a secret object and participate in a class discussion.

Learning Objective

Students will be able to guess the content of a secret science box correctly by orally asking science-related questions.

Materials

- box to hide a science object inside
- object that represents a new science unit of study

Procedure

1. Select an object that represents a new science unit you will be studying. For example, for a unit on matter, you may want to have a magnet. Keep the object hidden from students in a box.

2. Students guess the object in the box by asking you questions. Answer students' yes-or-no questions until they are able to guess the secret object.

3. Discuss the object after it is revealed.

Teacher Tip

- Use this activity at the beginning of every new science unit as a way to focus attention on the new theme. After several units, select a student or two to see the secret object you selected. These students should answer the other students' questions.

Differentiating by Proficiency Level

Beginning: Allow students to first question in their native languages and then ask them in English.

Intermediate: Encourage students to use complete sentences when discussing the object.

Advanced: Ask students to explain how their knowledge about the topic has changed.

> To differentiate by proficiency level, see pp. 11–15 for **Bloom's Taxonomy Questions** and pp. 19–24 for detailed examples.

Assessment

The following is a checklist of items to informally assess students after they complete this activity. Students should be able to:

- ask oral questions in order to guess the content of a secret science box

- practice listening skills by asking appropriate questions based on answers to previous questions

- participate in a classroom discussion pertaining to the science unit

Textures

Activity Length
Approximately
20–30 minutes

Activity Format
Whole group or
small groups

Standards

Grades K–2 (Science
Standard 13.1;
ELD Standard 2.2)

Grades 3–5 (Science
Standard 11.2;
ELD Standard 2.2)

Language Objective

Students will use English
to describe and sort
objects.

Learning Objective

Students will learn about
different textures and
sort objects into groups
according to their texture.

Materials

- objects with a variety of textures brought from home by students prior to the activity

- bath towel

Procedure

1. Ask each student to bring an object from home that has a special texture. (Send a note home requesting this.)

2. Ask students if they know what *texture* means. Discuss the meaning and show students examples of different textures in the classroom (the smooth top of a desk, the grainy sand, etc.).

3. Have students hide their objects under a towel one at a time.

4. Select students to take turns reaching under the towel and feel each object.

5. Encourage students to describe the texture (rough, smooth, sharp, prickly, soggy). Allow students to guess what the object is. Continue the process.

6. Sort objects into groups based on their textures.

Teacher Tip

- Use familiar objects with different textures from your own classroom.

Differentiating by Proficiency Level

Beginning: Use the whole-group format to allow students to hear the discussion.

Intermediate: Encourage students to tell more about their answers.

Advanced: Ask students to paraphrase what they have learned.

To differentiate by proficiency level, see pp. 11–15 for **Bloom's Taxonomy Questions** and pp. 19–24 for detailed examples.

Assessment

The following is a checklist of items to informally assess students after they complete this activity. Students should be able to:

- distinguish different textures

- describe objects with different textures

- sort objects into groups based on their texture

Three in a Row

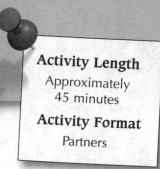

Activity Length
Approximately
45 minutes

Activity Format
Partners

Standards

Grades K–2 (Science
Standard 13.1;
ELD Standard 2.2)

Grades 3–5 (Science
Standard 11.2;
ELD Standard 2.2)

Language Objective

Students will use English
to practice vocabulary
by writing words and
listening for clues about
them.

Learning Objective

Students will reinforce
their knowledge of
forces and motion
by participating in a
traditional game.

Materials

- vocabulary words from the current science unit posted on a chart or on the board

- teacher-prepared sentences—one sentence that shows the meaning of each vocabulary word without using the word

- copies of page 111, one per student pair

Procedure

1. Distribute one copy of page 111 to each student. Have students work in pairs to write different vocabulary words from their science unit in the squares. For example, for a unit on forces and motion, you may have students write terms such as *magnet, gravity, repel, pull, force*, etc.

2. Read a sentence to students and ask them to put an *X* in the square when the word matches the sentence. For example, if the sentence read aloud was, "When Josh tried to place two magnets together, they would not link together," the pair would place an *X* in the square for *repel*. When a pair gets three *X*s in a row (horizontally, vertically, or diagonally), they call out, "Three in a row!" and they read back the words. Have students explain why the word works in the sentence.

Teacher Tips

- As an extended activity, have students create new sentences with the words.

- Have students draw a picture of the word to help with comprehension.

Differentiating by Proficiency Level

Beginning: Act out the meaning of each sentence as you say it.

Intermediate: Have students discuss answers with their partners.

Advanced: Ask students to explain how their knowledge about the topic has changed.

To differentiate by proficiency level, see pp. 11–15 for **Bloom's Taxonomy Questions** and pp. 19–24 for detailed examples.

Assessment

The following is a checklist of items to informally assess students after they complete this activity. Students should be able to:

- participate in a classroom discussion pertaining to the activity

- recognize correct usage of vocabulary terms

Three in a Row

Directions: Fill in the boxes with the science words your teacher gives you. Listen to each sentence. If the sentence tells about a word in a box, put an *X* in the box. When you get three *X*s in a row (horizontally, vertically, or diagonally), call out, "Three in a row!"

True/False Science

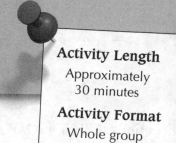

Standards

Grades K–2 (Science Standard 13.1; ELD Standard 2.2)

Grades 3–5 (Science Standard 11.2; ELD Standard 2.2)

Language Objective

Students will use English to listen to and determine whether statements are true or false. Students will learn the meaning of the terms true and false.

Learning Objective

Students will learn information about a current area of study.

Materials

- copies of page 113, one for each student
- scissors
- teacher-prepared list of statements about science theme

Procedure

1. Tell students that you are going to say some statements about the science theme you have been studying. Tell them some will be true and some will be false. Tell students it is their job to figure out which statements are true and which are false. Make sure students know the terms *true* and *false*.

2. Distribute copies of page 113. Have students cut out the cards. Tell them to place the cards in front of them.

3. Read one sentence statement. Have students work in pairs or small groups to discuss their answers. Students will then hold up the slip of paper they think is the correct answer. For example, if the statement read aloud was, "Scientists are done looking for fossils," students would hold up the statement paper they believe is the correct answer.

4. Select one student to tell the answer and reason why the statement is true or false. Continue with more statements.

Teacher Tip

- Allow students to make their own true/false statements. Give each student a chance to say a statement for others to respond to.

Differentiating by Proficiency Level

Beginning: Allow students to first discuss in their native languages and then respond in English.

Intermediate: Have students explain why answers were chosen.

Advanced: Ask students to paraphrase another students' response.

To differentiate by proficiency level, see pp. 11–15 for **Bloom's Taxonomy Questions** and pp. 19–24 for detailed examples.

Assessment

The following is a checklist of items to informally assess students after they complete this activity. Students should be able to:

- determine whether oral statements are true or false
- participate in a classroom discussion pertaining to the science theme

True/False Science

Directions: Cut out the true and false boxes. If a statement is true, hold up the "true" card. If a statement is false, hold up the "false" card.

True

False

Social Studies

This page is to keep a record of when the activities were taught and what adjustments or modifications were made. This log can be used to keep track of students' progress, to make modifications, and for future planning.

Activities	Notes
ABCs	
Famous People Similes	
Clothing Comparison	
Scavenger Hunt	
School Directions	
Secret Words	
State Riddles	
Telephone Role-Play	
Three in a Row	
Which Ocean, Which Continent?	

ABCs

Activity Length
Approximately
30–45 minutes

Activity Format
Whole group or
partners

Standards

Grades K–2 (Geography
Standard 5.1;
ELD Standard 2.2)

Grades 3–5 (Geography
Standard 5.1;
ELD Standard 2.2)

Language Objective

Students will use English
to participate in a
classroom discussion
about a social studies
theme.

Learning Objective

Students will have a
better understanding of
some vocabulary words
pertaining to regions.

Materials

- copies of page 116, one per student

Procedure

1. Discuss with students the social studies theme they are focussing on in class. Have a class discussion of what they might know about the topic and what they would like to know.

2. Distribute copies of page 116. Have students write the social studies topic in the center box. For example, if the theme that you are currently studying is regions, students would write *regions* in the Social Studies Topic box and fill in the chart according to the topic. The word *valley* could be placed under *V*, *desert* under *D*, and so on.

3. Discuss the answers that students wrote in their charts.

Teacher Tips

- The first time this activity is done, provide students with a word or two as examples before they participate.

- This activity can be used as a word wall. Enlarge the activity sheet so it can be placed in the classroom to help students have a better understanding of the new topic.

Differentiating by Proficiency Level

Beginning: Use the whole-group format to allow students to hear the discussion.

Intermediate: Ask students to say some words related to the topic.

Advanced: Ask students to defend and support their choices.

To differentiate by proficiency level, see pp. 11–15 for **Bloom's Taxonomy Questions** and pp. 19–24 for detailed examples.

Assessment

The following is a checklist of items to informally assess students after they complete this activity. Students should be able to:

- have a better understanding of the social studies theme

- participate in a classroom discussion pertaining to the social studies theme

Name: _____   Date: _____

ABCs

Directions: Think about the social studies topic. Write the social studies topic in the center box. Fill in the other boxes with words that start with the letter shown in each box.

A	B	C
D	**E**	**F**
G	**Social Studies Topic**	**H**
I		**J**
K		**L**
M		**N**
O	**P**	**Q**
R	**S**	**T**
U	**V**	**W**
X	**Y**	**Z**

Famous People Similes

Activity Length
Approximately
30 minutes

Activity Format
Partners

Standards

Grades K–2 (K–4 History Standard 4.2. 4.5–4.7; ELD Standard 2.2)

Grades 3–5 (K–4 History Standard 4.3; ELD Standard 2.2)

Language Objective

Students will use English to describe objects using similes.

Learning Objective

Students will learn information about famous people by using and sharing background knowledge to create similes.

Materials

- informational books about famous people in history
- chart paper

Procedure

1. Discuss the meaning of a simile with the class (comparing two things using the phrase "as___as___"). Give students social studies related examples such as, "George Washington's hair was as white as powder." "When George Washington went to war, he was as brave as a lion." Have students help create more examples of similes. Write their responses on the board.

2. Have students work in partners to create similes about a famous person in history. Before creating their similes, students should first research and learn information about a famous person in history.

3. As students are sharing their similes, write them on chart paper so students can compare them.

Teacher Tip

- Repeat this activity throughout the year as your class studies different famous people. Keep charts for comparisons.

Differentiating by Proficiency Level

Beginning: Provide choices for completing similes.
Intermediate: Have students explain their similes.
Advanced: Ask students to draw conclusions about the topic.

To differentiate by proficiency level, see pp. 11–15 for **Bloom's Taxonomy Questions** and pp. 19–24 for detailed examples.

Assessment

The following is a checklist of items to informally assess students after they complete this activity. Students should be able to:

- practice describing skills by using similes to describe objects
- develop grammar skills by creating similes using the form "as ___ as ___."

Clothing Comparison

Standards

Grades K–2 (K–4 History Standard 1.3; ELD Standard 2.2)

Grades 3–5 (K–4 History Standard 1.3; ELD Standard 2.2)

Language Objective

Students will use English to describe clothing and compare and contrast clothing now with clothing long ago.

Learning Objective

Students will know the cultural similarities and differences in clothes, homes, food, communication, technology, and cultural traditions between families now and in the past.

Materials

- assorted clothing from a time period you are studying (such as a waistcoat, knickers, bonnet, frock coat, hobble skirt, etc.) or photos of the clothing

Procedure

1. Show the historical clothing or the photos to the class. Discuss the time period of the clothing you are studying.

2. Show each piece of clothing (or photo). Take time to discuss it. Encourage students to describe it in as much detail as possible.

3. Continue the process with other clothing pieces. Compare the clothing with today's clothing.

Teacher Tip

- For future activities, use clothing from a specific country or culture the class has been studying.

Differentiating by Proficiency Level

Beginning: Ask students to point to the historical clothes as they say their names.

Intermediate: Build students' vocabulary by providing additional vocabulary to describe the clothing.

Advanced: Ask students to explain how their knowledge about the topic has changed.

To differentiate by proficiency level, see pp. 11–15 for **Bloom's Taxonomy Questions** and pp. 19–24 for detailed examples.

Assessment

The following is a checklist of items to informally assess students after they complete this activity. Students should be able to:

- have a better understanding of a time period after discussing assorted clothing pieces from a historical time
- follow verbal directions by correctly modeling how to wear the historical clothing

Scavenger Hunt

Standards

Grades K–2 (K–4 History
Standard 7.1;
ELD Standard 2.2)

Grades 3–5 (K–4 History
Standard 7.5;
ELD Standard 2.2)

Language Objective

Students will use
English to talk together
and search for new
information. Students
will orally share
information.

Learning Objective

Students will develop
categorization and
vocabulary skills by
working cooperatively
and communicating
effectively in small
groups.

Materials

- Real objects (realia), magazines, maps, and other publications with pictures related to your current social studies topic

- copies of a teacher-prepared scavenger hunt list, one per group

Procedure

1. Discuss with the class what a scavenger hunt is (a game where people find a variety of items on a list). Tell students they will be working in groups to find a list of objects or pictures related to the current social studies theme. For example, if you are currently studying world cultures, have students look for various objects that represent various parts of the world.

2. Divide the class into groups. Give each group a copy of the scavenger hunt list you have created. Students will work together to find as many pictures or objects as possible from the list.

3. Have groups show and tell about the scavenger hunt items they found.

Teacher Tip

- Repeat this activity with different social studies themes throughout the year. Allow students to create scavenger hunt lists for the rest of the class.

Differentiating by Proficiency Level

Beginning: Preview the list with students in a small group.
Intermediate: During the discussion at the end of the activity ask students to say other words related to the topic.
Advanced: Ask students to defend and support their choices.

To differentiate by proficiency level, see pp. 11–15 for **Bloom's Taxonomy Questions** and pp. 19–24 for detailed examples.

Assessment

The following is a checklist of items to informally assess students after they complete this activity. Students should be able to:

- search for information in different sources

- orally share information about their findings

- work cooperatively in finding the various objects

School Directions

Standards

Grades K–2 (Geography
Standard 2.1;
ELD Standard 2.2)

Grades 3–5 (Geography
Standard 2.1;
ELD Standard 2.2)

Language Objective

Students will use English
to listen to and give
directions.

Learning Objective

Students will develop
basic map skills by giving
and receiving accurate
oral directions of a map.

Materials

- copies of page 121, one per student

Procedure

1. Distribute copies of page 121. Tell students to listen carefully while you tell them how to get from one place to another on the map. For example, you might say, "Go through the front door and go into the third room on the left. Where are you?" (Answer: second grade room.) Give another direction, such as, "Start in the cafeteria. Go to the side of the cafeteria that is opposite from the kitchen. Then go into the door closest to the stage. Where are you?" (Answer: art room.)

2. After you give several directions with the school map, have students work with partners. Each pair should have a map. Partners should take turns giving each other directions to follow on the map.

Teacher Tip

- Have students create a map of your school. Encourage students to explore your school and draw the map as accurately as possible. (If you have a large school, you may wish to limit the map to one floor or area.)

Differentiating by Proficiency Level

Beginning: Give students directions one at a time.

Intermediate: Encourage students to ask for clarification on any direction if needed.

Advanced: Pair up advanced students and encourage them to use more complex language structures in their directions.

To differentiate by proficiency level, see pp. 11–15 for **Bloom's Taxonomy Questions** and pp. 19–24 for detailed examples.

Assessment

The following is a checklist of items to informally assess students after they complete this activity. Students should be able to:

- develop a basic map

- reinforce vocabulary pertaining to directions (right, left, below, above, etc.)

- follow oral directions

- work cooperatively in partners to give each other several directions about the school map

School Directions

Directions: Listen carefully as your partner tells you exactly where to move your fingers on the map.

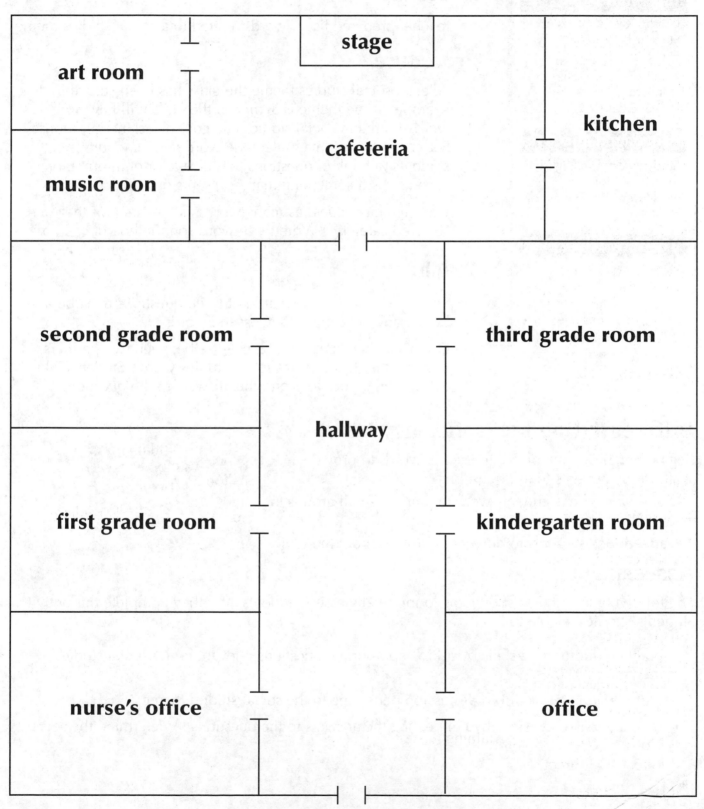

stage

art room

music roon

cafeteria

kitchen

second grade room

third grade room

hallway

first grade room

kindergarten room

nurse's office

office

 #50203—Activities for English Language Learners Across the Curriculum

Secret Words

Standards

Grades K–2 (K–4 History Standard 4.8; ELD Standard 2.2)

Grades 3–5 (K–4 History Standard 4.11; ELD Standard 2.2)

Language Objective

Students will use English to ask questions and guess words belonging to a category.

Learning Objective

Students will improve their knowledge of American symbols by asking questions relevant to the theme.

Materials

- teacher-prepared list of words related to a social studies theme

Procedure

1. Select a social studies theme the class has been studying. For example, if the theme is *Symbols*, the class will have to guess words from that social studies category by asking questions. For example, you may select the word *flag*. Encourage students to think of questions that give a lot of information, such as, "Is it something that represents our country?"

2. Have the class guess as many words as they can for the selected category. Write these words on the board.

Teacher Tips

- Set a rule that states that at least three questions must be asked before anyone can try to guess the word.

- Do this activity as a writing exercise between two partners. Each partner has a secret social studies word. Students take turns writing questions and the answers to the questions.

Differentiating by Proficiency Level

Beginning: Show pictures of the secret words to provide a scaffold for students to ask questions.

Intermediate: Have students work in pairs or small groups to discuss their questions.

Advanced: Ask students to draw conclusions about the topic.

> To differentiate by proficiency level, see pp. 11–15 for **Bloom's Taxonomy Questions** and pp. 19–24 for detailed examples.

Assessment

The following is a checklist of items to informally assess students after they complete this activity. Students should be able to:

- practice questioning skills by asking appropriate questions relevant to the social studies theme

- participate in a classroom discussion pertaining to the social studies theme

- practice reasoning skills by connecting the answers to the questions to determine the secret word

State Riddles

Activity Length
Approximately
45 minutes

Activity Format
Whole group or
small groups

Standards

Grades K–2 (K–4 History
Standard 3.0;
ELD Standard 2.2)

Grades 3–5 (K–4 History
Standard 3.0;
ELD Standard 2.2)

Language Objective

Students will use English
to create riddles and
share them.

Learning Objective

Students will use
knowledge about states to
create oral riddles.

Materials

- 3"x 5" lined index cards
- construction paper, one sheet per student
- crayons or markers for each student

Procedure

1. After students have studied a variety of U.S. states (or cities or states in the country they live in), have them create state riddles for the rest of the class to guess the answers.

2. Each student selects one state and keeps it a secret.

3. After selecting their state, students fold a sheet of construction paper in half and draw a picture or write the name of their state on the inside of their folded construction paper. On the outside of the construction paper, each student writes three or four facts about the state. For example, a card might read:

   - I became a state in 1820.
   - My state bird is the Chickadee.
   - My nickname is the Pine Tree State.
   - What state am I? (Maine)

4. After students finish making their riddle cards, have them take turns sharing their riddles.

Teacher Tips

- Try to have a map of the different states as a visual.
- The first time this activity is done, place students into small groups.

Differentiating by Proficiency Level

Beginning: Give students simple sentence frames to complete.
Intermediate: Ask students to use complete sentences when creating their riddles.
Advanced: Encourage students to use academic language in their written responses.

To differentiate by proficiency level, see pp. 11–15 for **Bloom's Taxonomy Questions** and pp. 19–24 for detailed examples.

Assessment

The following is a checklist of items to informally assess students after they complete this activity. Students should be able to:

- accurately give oral descriptions about U.S. states
- reinforce vocabulary about the knowledge of U.S. states

Telephone Role-Play

Activity Length
Approximately 30–45 minutes

Activity Format
Whole group

Standards

Grades K–2 (K–4 History Standard 8.5; ELD Standard 3.1)

Grades 3–5 (K–4 History Standard 8.5; ELD Standard 3.1)

Language Objective

Students will use English to role-play a telephone conversation.

Learning Objective

Students will learn about communication and compare communication now with communication long ago.

Materials

- phone book
- unconnected phone
- copy of page 125, cut into individual slips

Procedure

1. Compare how people communicated a long time ago to how they communicate today.

2. Tell the class that they will be role-playing using the telephone. One student at a time pulls a slip of paper containing a telephone role-play situation and reads it aloud.

3. That student looks up the correct number in the phone book, calls that number on the unconnected phone and role-plays the phone call described on the slip of paper. Pretend to be the person on the other line.

4. Before beginning the calls, lead a class discussion on phone etiquette.

5. Since you will be role-playing a part in every phone call, stand near the student "making the call."

Teacher Tip

- You may not get to every student in one class. Carry this activity over to the next day or when you have a few extra minutes at the end of a class.

Differentiating by Proficiency Level

Beginning: Allow students to act out their responses.

Intermediate: Encourage students to answer in complete sentences.

Advanced: Ask students to create their own examples of the activity.

To differentiate by proficiency level, see pp. 11–15 for **Bloom's Taxonomy Questions** and pp. 19–24 for detailed examples.

Assessment

The following is a checklist of items to informally assess students after they complete this activity. Students should be able to:

- develop role-playing skills by pretending to make a telephone call
- develop social communication skills by role-playing a telephone conversation

Telephone Role-Play

Directions: Copy this page and cut along the lines. You may wish to write some of your own telephone role-play situations.

Your teacher wants you to call the bus station to see what time the bus will be arriving to pick you up.	Call the public library to see what time they close today.
Call the post office to see what time they close on Saturday.	Call a pizza place to order five large cheese pizzas for the class.
Call the police station to report that your bike has been stolen.	Call the school to say that your father has a flat tire so he will be late bringing you to school today.
Call the phone company to report that your home phone is not working.	Call the airport to see what time the last flight of the day arrives.
Your mom asks you to call city hall to see what date property taxes are due.	Call a pet store to see if they sell rabbits.
Call a car wash to see if they are open 24 hours a day.	Call a bank to see what their Saturday hours are.
Call a car dealership to see if they have any used Volkswagen cars for sale.	Call a bus station to see if they offer service to Boston.
Call a taxi to pick you up at school and bring you home.	Call a movie theater to see what movies are playing.
Call an animal shelter to see if they have had a calico cat brought in.	Your mother asks you to call a disposal service to see what their rates are for trash removal.
Call the nearest mall to see what time they open on Sunday.	Call a zoo or animal park to see if they have any Pandas.

Three in a Row

Activity Length
Approximately
45 minutes

Activity Format
Whole group

Standards

Grades K–2 (Civics
Standard 3.6;
ELD Standard 2.2)

Grades 3–5 (Civics
Standard 3.1;
ELD Standard 2.2)

Language Objective

Students will use English
to practice vocabulary
by writing words and
listening for clues about
them.

Learning Objective

Students will reinforce
their knowledge
of vocabulary by
participating in a
traditional game.

Materials

- vocabulary words from the current social studies theme

- teacher-prepared sentences—one sentence that shows the meaning of each vocabulary word without using the word

- copies of page 127, one per student pair

Procedure

1. Distribute one copy of page 127 to each student. Have students write different social studies vocabulary words in the squares. For example, for a unit on civics, you may have students write terms such as *fair, equal, rule, law, security*, etc.

2. Read a sentence to students and ask them to put an *X* in the square when the word matches the sentence. For example, if the sentence read aloud was, "He needed to follow what the police officer told him to do, or else he would be breaking this," the student would place an *X* in the square for *law*. When a student gets three *X*s (horizontally, vertically, or diagonally), they call out, "Three in a row!" and the game is over.

Teacher Tips

- As an extended activity, have students create new sentences with the vocabulary words.

- Have students draw a picture of the word to help with comprehension.

Differentiating by Proficiency Level

Beginning: Act out the meaning of each sentence as you say it.
Intermediate: Have students discuss answers with their partners.
Advanced: Ask students to explain how their knowledge about the topic has changed.

To differentiate by proficiency level, see pp. 11–15 for **Bloom's Taxonomy Questions** and pp. 19–24 for detailed examples.

Assessment

The following is a checklist of items to informally assess students after they complete this activity. Students should be able to:

- write selected vocabulary words

- recognize correct usage of vocabulary terms

Three in a Row

Directions: Fill in the boxes with social studies words your teacher gives you. Listen to the sentence. If the sentence tells about a word in a box, put an *X* in the box. When you get three *X*s in a row (horizontally, vertically, or diagonally), call out, "Three in a row!"

Which Ocean, Which Continent?

Activity Length
Approximately 30 minutes

Activity Format
Whole group

Standards

Grades K–2 (Geography Standard 2.1;
ELD Standard 2.2)

Grades 3–5 (Geography Standard 2.3;
ELD Standard 2.2)

Language Objective

Students will use English to give and follow directions.

Learning Objective

Students will have a better understanding about the oceans and continents by correctly using a map of the world to identify specific locations.

Materials

- copies of page 129, one per student

Procedure

1. Distribute copies of page 129. Tell students they will be playing a guessing game with the maps by giving and following directions about oceans and continents.

2. Review with students the names and locations of the oceans and continents.

3. Tell students to listen carefully to your directions, to follow them exactly, and then to guess the "secret" ocean or continent. Give directions such as, "Put your finger in the middle of Australia and then move it west. Which ocean do you come to? (Answer: Indian Ocean.)

4. Continue with more directions.

Teacher Tips

- As a follow up, have students do this activity with partners taking turns giving each other ocean and continent directions.

- To reinforce writing skills and accuracy, have students write ocean and continent directions for students to read and follow.

Differentiating by Proficiency Level

Beginning: Repeat key vocabulary words in a systematic way.

Intermediate: Have students explain how they determined their answers.

Advanced: Encourage students to use academic language when giving directions to their partners.

To differentiate by proficiency level, see pp. 11–15 for **Bloom's Taxonomy Questions** and pp. 19–24 for detailed examples.

Assessment

The following is a checklist of items to informally assess students after they complete this activity. Students should be able to:

- follow oral directions by correctly using the map to find answers to questions orally given

- reinforce vocabulary pertaining to directions (right, left, below, above, etc.)

Name: _____   Date: _____

Which Ocean, Which Continent?

Directions: Listen carefully to the directions to tell you exactly where to move your fingers on the map.

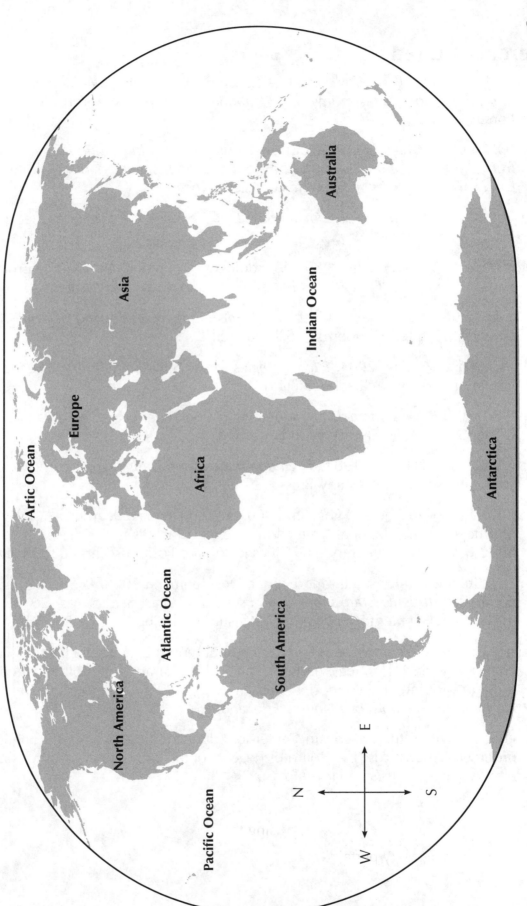

References Cited

Anderson, L., and D.E. Krathwohl. 2001. *A taxonomy for learning teaching and assessing: A revision of Bloom's taxonomy of educational objectives.* New York: AddisonWesley Longman, Inc.

August, D., and T. Shanahan, Eds. 2006. *Developing literacy in second-language learners: Lessons from the report of the National Literacy Panel on language-minority children and youth.* Mahwah, NJ: Lawrence Erlbaum Associates, Inc.

Bloom, B. S. 1956. *Taxonomy of educational objectives: The classification of educational goals.* Vol. 1. New York: McKay.

Collier, V. P., and W. P. Thomas. 1989. How quickly can immigrants become proficient in school English? *Journal of Educational Issues of Language Minority Students* 5:26–38.

Graddol, D. 2006. English next: *Why global English may mean the end of 'English as a foreign language'.* United Kingdom: British Council.

Herrell, A., and M. Jordan. 2004. *Fifty strategies for teaching English language learners.* 2nd ed. Upper Saddle, NJ: Pearson Education, Inc.

Jimenez, E. 2009. *Raising the achievement level of English language learners through SDAIE.* Upper Saddle River, NJ: Pearson Education, Inc.

Krashen, S. D., and T. Terrell. 1983. *The natural approach: Language acquisition in the classroom.* San Francisco, CA: Alemany Press.

National Council of Teachers of English. 2008. English language learners: A policy research brief produced by the National Council of Teachers of English. http://www.ncte.org/library/NCTEFiles/Resources/Positions/Chron0308PolicyBrief.pdf

National Institute of Child Health and Human Development. 2006. *Public elementary and secondary students, staff, schools, and school districts: School year 2003–2004.* Report of the National Center for Educational Statistics. Washington, DC: ED Pubs.

Ramirez, J. D. 1992. Executive summary of the final report: Longitudinal study of structured English immersion strategy, early-exit and late-exit transitional bilingual education programs for language minority children. *Bilingual Research Journal: The Journal of the National Association for Bilingual Education, 16.*

WIDA—housed within the Wisconsin Center for Education Research. 2007. English language proficiency standards. The Board of Regents of the University of Wisconsin System, http://www.wida.us/standards/elp.aspx.

Student Reproducibles

Page	Title	Filename
Reading		
34	ABCs	abcreading.pdf
38	Fill in the Squares	fillin.pdf
40	Bright Idea	bright.pdf
45	Study an Author	study.pdf
47	Three in a Row	threeinarowreading.pdf
49	Tricky Word Flags	wordflags.pdf
Writing		
53	ABCs	abcwriting.pdf
57	Name It!	nameit.pdf
61	Change the Words	change.pdf
66	So-Close Pictures	soclose.pdf
68	The Fewest Clues	fewest.pdf
70	Idiom Pictures	idiom.pdf
72	Word Changes	wordchanges.pdf
Mathematics		
76	ABCs	abcmath.pdf
79	Three in a Row	threeinarowmath.pdf
82	Math Words	mathwords.pdf
84	Let Your Fingers Do the Walking on the Calendar	calendar.pdf
87	Math High Five	hand.pdf
90	Math King/Queen	kingqueen.pdf
93	Time Directions	time.pdf
Science		
96	ABCs	abcscience.pdf
99	Bingo	bingo.pdf
101	Science Maze	maze.pdf
105	Science Synonyms	synonyms.pdf
107	Science Vocabulary	vocabulary.pdf
111	Three in a Row	threeinarowscience.pdf
113	True/False Science	truefalse.pdf
Social Studies		
116	ABCs	abcss.pdf
121	School Directions	directions.pdf
125	Telephone Role-Play	roleplay.pdf
127	Three in a Row	threeinarowss.pdf
129	Which Ocean, Which Continent?	ocean.pdf

Teacher Resource Pages

Page	Title	Filename
8–9	Proficiency Levels at a Quick Glance	quickglance.pdf
11–15	Proficiency Questions	proficiencyq.pdf
20	Example Lesson by Proficiency Level (Beginning)	beginning.pdf
21	Example Lesson by Proficiency Level (Early Intermediate)	eintermediate.pdf
22	Example Lesson by Proficiency Level (Intermediate)	intermediate.pdf
23	Example Lesson by Proficiency Level (Early Advanced)	eadvanced.pdf
24	Example Lesson by Proficiency Level (Advanced)	advanced.pdf
32	Activities Log (Reading)	reading.pdf
51	Activities Log (Writing)	writing.pdf
74	Activities Log (Mathematics)	mathematics.pdf
94	Activities Log (Science)	science.pdf
114	Activities Log (Social Studies)	socialstudies.pdf

Notes